The Rise of the Roman Empire

Other Books in the Turning Points Series:

Turning Points

IN WORLD HISTORY

The Rise of the Roman Empire

Don Nardo, *Book Editor*

Daniel Leone, *Publisher*
Bonnie Szumski, *Editorial Director*
Scott Barbour, *Managing Editor*

Greenhaven Press, Inc., San Diego, California

Every effort has been made to trace the owners of copyrighted material. The articles in this volume may have been edited for content, length, and/or reading level. The titles have been changed to enhance the editorial purpose.

No part of this book may be reproduced or used in any form or by any means, electrical, mechanical, or otherwise, including, but not limited to, photocopy, recording, or any information storage and retrieval system, without prior written permission from the publisher.

Library of Congress Cataloging-in-Publication Data

The rise of the Roman Empire / Don Nardo, book editor.
    p. cm. — (Turning points in world history)
  Includes bibliographical references and index.
  ISBN 0-7377-0756-9 (pbk. : alk. paper)—
ISBN 0-7377-0757-7 (lib. : alk. paper)
    1. Rome—History—To 510 B.C. 2. Rome—History—Republic, 510–30 B.C. I. Nardo, Don, 1947– II. Turning points in world history (Greenhaven Press)

DG231 .R57 2002
937'.02—dc21   2001033512
                                      CIP

© 2002 by Greenhaven Press, Inc.
10911 Technology Place, San Diego, CA 92127

Printed in the U.S.A.

Contents

its military system, which underwent a major overhaul in the fourth century B.C. After this, its army was the most flexible and effective in the known world.

Chapter 3: The Punic Wars

Foreword

Certain past events stand out as pivotal, as having effects and outcomes that change the course of history. These events are often referred to as turning points. Historian Louis L. Snyder provides this useful definition:

> A turning point in history is an event, happening, or stage which thrusts the course of historical development into a different direction. By definition a turning point is a great event, but it is even more—a great event with the explosive impact of altering the trend of man's life on the planet.

History's turning points have taken many forms. Some were single, brief, and shattering events with immediate and obvious impact. The invasion of Britain by William the Conqueror in 1066, for example, swiftly transformed that land's political and social institutions and paved the way for the rise of the modern English nation. By contrast, other single events were deemed of minor significance when they occurred, only later recognized as turning points. The assassination of a little-known European nobleman, Archduke Franz Ferdinand, on June 28, 1914, in the Bosnian town of Sarajevo was such an event; only after it touched off a chain reaction of political-military crises that escalated into the global conflict known as World War I did the murder's true significance become evident.

Other crucial turning points occurred not in terms of a few hours, days, months, or even years, but instead as evolutionary developments spanning decades or even centuries. One of the most pivotal turning points in human history, for instance—the development of agriculture, which replaced nomadic hunter-gatherer societies with more permanent settlements—occurred over the course of many generations. Still other great turning points were neither events nor developments, but rather revolutionary new inventions and innovations that significantly altered social customs and ideas, military tactics, home life, the spread of knowledge, and the human condition in general. The developments of writing, gunpowder, the printing press, antibiotics, the electric light, atomic energy, television, and the computer, the last two of which have recently ushered in the world-altering information age, represent only some of these innovative turning points.

Each anthology in the Greenhaven Turning Points in World History series presents a group of essays chosen for their accessibility. The anthology's structure also enhances this accessibility. First, an introductory essay provides a general overview of the principal events and figures involved, placing the topic in its historical context. The essays that follow explore various aspects in more detail, some targeting political trends and consequences, others social, literary, cultural, and/or technological ramifications, and still others pivotal leaders and other influential figures. To aid the reader in choosing the material of immediate interest or need, each essay is introduced by a concise summary of the contributing writer's main themes and insights.

In addition, each volume contains extensive research tools, including a collection of excerpts from primary source documents pertaining to the historical events and figures under discussion. In the anthology on the French Revolution, for example, readers can examine the works of Rousseau, Voltaire, and other writers and thinkers whose championing of human rights helped fuel the French people's growing desire for liberty; the French *Declaration of the Rights of Man and Citizen*, presented to King Louis XVI by the French National Assembly on October 2, 1789; and eyewitness accounts of the attack on the royal palace and the horrors of the Reign of Terror. To guide students interested in pursuing further research on the subject, each volume features an extensive bibliography, which for easy access has been divided into separate sections by topic. Finally, a comprehensive index allows readers to scan and locate content efficiently. Each of the anthologies in the Greenhaven Turning Points in World History series provides students with a complete, detailed, and enlightening examination of a crucial historical watershed.

Introduction: Rome's Foundation and Rise to Greatness

The ancient city-state—and later the sprawling empire—of Rome changed the face of Italy, Europe, and the Mediterranean world forever. Before the Romans began their momentous rise to power, no single people dominated all or even most of that world. In the early years of the first millennium B.C., a high civilization developed in Greece, one whose culture would profoundly influence that of Rome in subsequent centuries. Various Greek city-states developed, some of which established colonies on distant Mediterranean coasts. But none of these political entities gained lasting power over wide sections of the Mediterranean. In the east, meanwhile, Egypt and Palestine came under the sway of the Assyrians, Babylonians, and later the Persians (whose realms were centered in what is now Iraq and Iran); the North African coast was settled by a maritime people, the Phoenicians, who established the great city of Carthage there; and most of the still-dense forests of Europe were sparsely inhabited by Celtic tribesmen who lacked both cities and the ability to write.

In these same centuries, the Romans were merely one of a large number of local peoples inhabiting various sections of Italy. In fact, they began as one of the least powerful and more culturally backward of these peoples. Yet between the sixth and second centuries B.C.—a relatively brief period of about four centuries—the Romans burst forth from obscurity in their tiny homeland, conquered all of Italy, laid Carthage low, overran the Greeks, and gained control of most of southern Europe.

Had Rome not risen to Mediterranean mastery, it is certain that the Greeks, Carthaginians, or perhaps someone else would have filled that power vacuum. And the fate and subsequent histories of Europe and the lands surrounding it would have been significantly different. As it was, though, Rome remained the dominant power in that sector of the world for another seven centuries; and its language, customs, and ideas profoundly transfigured Europe long after the Roman Empire fell in the fifth and sixth centuries. Therefore, the rise of Rome was, like its fall, one of the great turning points in world history.

The Nature of the Evidence

Piecing together the story of Rome's early centuries is not an easy task, to be sure. This is because of the nature of the evidence, which is of two major kinds. The first consists of ancient literary sources, books written by historians and other ancient writers. The two most important of these sources for early Rome are the histories of a Roman, Livy, and a Greek, Dionysius of Halicarnassus. The problem is that both men lived and wrote in the late first century B.C. And as T.J. Cornell, a noted expert on early Rome, says, their works "were all written centuries after the events they describe, which inevitably raises the question of how historical they really are."[1] The fact is that Livy and other ancient historians conducted little or no independent research of their own. Instead, they tended mainly to repeat and pass on information from previous writers, some of them fairly reliable but others extremely *un*reliable. The result was that many of the original facts were distorted or even replaced by fabrications over the course of time. Therefore, modern scholars must be very careful and discerning in their use of such ancient texts.

The second major kind of evidence relating to early Rome is that provided by archaeologists, scholars who dig up and study past civilizations. Archaeology provided a great deal of information on the subject during the twentieth century, especially in its last twenty-five years. Most of the surviving evidence is in the form of artifacts and inscriptions found in scattered graves and tombs. This is because the vast majority of Roman houses and other buildings from the early first millennium B.C., along with their contents, have long since disappeared. By contrast, far more is known about Rome's later centuries, which left behind numerous stone structures, sculptures, pottery containers, coins, and other artifacts. Still, though the evidence for Rome's early centuries is fragmentary, enough of it has been uncovered to piece together at least a general picture of those centuries. "The evidence is indeed extremely difficult," Cornell admits, "and problems of verification [of the facts] are acute, but it is incorrect to say that nothing can be known about how Rome began, or how it developed during the early centuries of its existence."[2]

Certainly, whatever the combination of literary and archaeological sources can tell about early Rome and its rise to greatness is of major interest, not only to historians but to everyone. Besides the fact that the rise of Rome is of historical significance, there is the natural curiosity people throughout the ages have had about the most successful and powerful among them. Today, that curiosity is most often manifested in the proliferation of popular books and films about the rise of powerful nations such as England and the United States and the kings, presidents, and other leaders who shaped them. In ancient times, Rome was most often the subject of such interest and scrutiny. The second-century-B.C. Greek historian Polybius summed it up well in the introduction to his history of Rome, writing,

> The events I have chosen to describe will challenge and stimulate everyone alike, both young and old, to study my systematic history. There can surely be nobody so petty or so apathetic in his outlook that he has no desire to discover by what means and under what system of government the Romans succeeded in . . . bringing under their rule almost the whole of the inhabited world, an achievement which is without parallel in human history.[3]

Two Versions of Rome's Beginnings

The amount of evidence modern scholars have about Rome's beginnings is a good deal larger than what was available to Polybius. What does that evidence, especially recent archaeological finds, reveal about the original founding of the so-called eternal city? First, the famous version of the founding accepted by the Romans themselves was undoubtedly too simplistic and dated too late. In the first century B.C., during Rome's literary golden age, several Roman scholars tried to arrive at an exact founding date. This was a difficult task because over the centuries the Romans had used several different calendars and dating systems, which contained various inconsistencies and omissions. Eventually, a noted scholar of the day, Marcus Terentius Varro (who died in 27 B.C.), calculated what was thereafter the most widely accepted date—753 B.C.[4] In that year, the story went, the hero Romulus established Rome on the Palatine, one of the seven low hills on which the city subsequently grew.

Contrary to this legendary scenario, modern archaeology has revealed that Rome and its society and culture did not appear nearly as suddenly; rather, it developed slowly over the course of many centuries. Evidence shows that the group of Latin-speaking tribes to which the Romans belonged lived in Italy long before the eighth century B.C. Moreover, there was likely no single, purposeful founding of Rome. Instead, the city's site was long occupied by primitive villages, which gradually came together to form one town. The Roman founding myths may have been based on garbled memories of real people and events from Rome's earliest centuries. So as they continue to unearth new knowledge about these obscure times, archaeologists and historians remain mindful that Roman mythology and history are probably intricately intertwined in ways that are still not well understood.

Rome's story has two beginnings, therefore, each of which must be considered in the context of the other. The first is the one accepted by the ancient Romans themselves; the other is the one revealed by the spades of modern excavators. In their own version, the Romans, like all peoples in all ages, wanted to believe that they were descended from characters of heroic stature. They took note that the Greeks, whose culture they admired and eagerly absorbed, looked back with pride to their ancestors' exploits in the remote and legendary "Age of Heroes." (Historians now identify this era with the late Greek Bronze Age, ca. 1400–1150 B.C.)

A Link with the Trojan War

Especially important to the Greeks was the Trojan War. In this epic tale, later immortalized by the Greek poet Homer in his *Iliad*, a number of early Greek kings banded together in an expedition against the prosperous city of Troy, located on the northwestern coast of Asia Minor, what is now Turkey. Following a long siege, they destroyed the city and recovered Helen, a Greek queen who had been abducted by a Trojan prince. The heroes of that conflict, including the Greeks Achilles and Odysseus and the Trojans Hector and Aeneas, were seen as men of larger-than-life stature who accomplished deeds of incredible valor and interacted with the gods. When Greek settlers began establishing cities in southern Italy in the late 700s and early 600s B.C., they brought their legends of the Trojan War with them.

The early Romans, who inhabited a nearby small patch of central Italy, soon had sporadic contact with the more culturally advanced visitors and were duly impressed. Perhaps because they had no ancestral heroes of their own who compared with those who fought at Troy, the Romans attempted to create a link between themselves and one of the leading characters of the Trojan story. At least by the sixth century B.C., it appears, Roman legends had incorporated the tale of the Trojan prince Aeneas's escape from the burning Troy and his fateful journey to Italy.

The major ancient version of Aeneas's story was *The Aeneid*, an epic poem composed by the first-century-B.C. Roman writer Virgil. Following several dangerous and colorful adventures, Virgil wrote, the hero sailed to Cumae, on Italy's southwestern coast. A prophet had earlier advised him to seek out the Sibyl, a wise woman who could see into the future. When Aeneas found her, she greeted him and told him that he was destined to fight a war in Italy over the right to marry an Italian bride. He then begged her to help him find a way into the underworld so that he could once more see his beloved father, Anchises, who had died during the long journey across the Mediterranean. Granting the request, the Sibyl led Aeneas down into the underworld and in time they found the spirit of the old man.

After Aeneas and Anchises were reunited, the father showed his son the future of the noble and blessed race Aeneas would sire. "I shall show you the whole span of our destiny," said Anchises (according to Virgil). First, the old man's spirit revealed that Aeneas's offspring would establish the city of Alba Longa in the Italian region of Latium (lying south of the Tiber River). And the line of Alba's noble rulers would lead to Romulus, who himself would establish a city—none other than Rome. "Under his tutelage," Anchises predicted, "our glorious Rome shall rule the whole wide world [and] her spirit shall match the spirit of the gods."[5] Anchises showed his son the long line of noble Romans, finally culminating in the greatest of them all, Augustus Caesar, who was destined to bring about a new golden age for Rome and humanity. (In fact, it was Augustus, Virgil's friend, who established the Roman Empire in the late first century B.C.)

Eventually, the Sibyl led Aeneas back up to the earth's surface. The hero then traveled northward to Latium to fulfill the destiny that had been revealed to him. He met the local ruler, Latinus, and soon sought the hand of that king's daughter, Lavinia. But Turnus, the prince of a neighboring people called the Rutulians, had already asked for Lavinia's hand, and the rivalry over Lavinia soon led to a terrible war. This proved to be the fulfillment of the Sibyl's prophecy that Aeneas would fight over an Italian bride.

The conflict dragged on for some time, and many people died on both sides. But finally Aeneas managed to defeat Turnus and marry Lavinia. From the union of the Trojan and Latin races, fulfilling the destiny ordained by Jupiter, leader of the gods, sprang the lineage that would lead to the noble Romans, who would one day rule all the world. For the Romans, Jupiter had told the love goddess Venus, "I see no measure nor date [and] I grant them dominion without end . . . the master-race, the wearers of the Toga. So it is willed!"[6]

Romulus Establishes a City

Thus, the Romans tied Romulus, the hero of their most popular local founding legend, to the Trojan hero Aeneas through family lineage. Romulus and his twin brother, Remus, were supposedly members of the royal house of Alba Longa. When they were infants, their great-uncle, who had usurped the throne, ordered them to be drowned in the

Tiber; but they fortunately washed ashore, where a she-wolf fed them and some poor shepherds eventually took them in. When the brothers grew to manhood and learned their true identities, they returned to Alba, overthrew their great-uncle, and restored their grandfather, the rightful king, to his throne. Then they set out to establish a new city of their own on the northern edge of the Latium plain.

Romulus ended up establishing the city by himself, however, for he and Remus got into a petty squabble, fought, and Romulus slew his brother. Shortly after this tragedy, Romulus laid the new town's initial foundations, as told by the first-century-A.D. Greek writer Plutarch in his biography of Romulus:

> Having buried his brother Remus . . . [Romulus] set to building his city; and sent for men out of Tuscany [then Etruria, homeland of the Etruscans], who directed him . . . in all the ceremonies to be observed, as in a religious rite. First, they dug a round trench . . . and into it solemnly threw the first-fruits of all things either good by custom or necessary by nature; lastly, every man taking a small piece of earth of the country from whence he came, they all threw [the piece] in randomly together. Making this trench . . . their center, they laid out the boundary of the city in a circle round it. Then the founder fitted to a plow a metal plowshare [blade], and, yoking together a bull and a cow, drove himself a deep line or furrow round the boundary. . . . With this line they laid out the [city] wall [on the Palatine, one of Rome's famed seven hills]; and where they designed to make a gate, there they . . . left a space. . . . As for the day they began to build the city, it is universally agreed to have been the twenty-first of April, and that day the Romans annually keep holy, calling it their country's birthday. At first, they say, they sacrificed [to the gods] no living creature on this day, thinking it fit to preserve the feast of their country's birthday pure and without stain of blood.[7]

Once he had established Rome, Romulus proceeded immediately to deal with some important religious, legal, and social matters. According to Livy, after building his wall on the Palatine,

> he offered sacrifice to the gods. . . . Having performed with

proper ceremony his religious duties, he summoned his subjects and gave them laws. . . . Meanwhile Rome was growing.
. . . To help fill his big new town, [Romulus] threw open . . . a
place of asylum for fugitives. Hither fled for refuge all the [out-
casts] from the neighboring peoples; some free, some slaves,
and all of them wanting nothing more than a fresh start.[8]

Romulus's welcoming of foreigners into the city, like the
non-Italian origins of Aeneas, was among later Romans' attempts to explain the cosmopolitan nature of their state.
"The Roman foundation legend," T.J. Cornell writes,

provides evidence, first and foremost, of how the Romans of
later times chose to see themselves. . . . The most revealing
sign of this is the way it defines the identity of the Roman
people as a mixture of different ethnic groups, and of Roman
culture as the product of various foreign influences. . . . The
Roman saga was characteristic of a people who had built up
their power by extending their citizenship and continuously
admitting new elements into their midst.[9]

Scholars Search for the First Romans

The natural question is to what extent do the events of this
foundation myth about Romulus match the findings made in
Italy by modern scholars? First, in the 1930s the remains of
the bases of some primitive huts were discovered on the Palatine and tentatively dated to the eighth century B.C. Both the
site and period are the same as those mentioned in the chief
myth of Romulus. Furthermore, more recently, archaeologists have found evidence that one particular hut remained in
good repair for many centuries, coexisting with, rather than
being replaced by, larger stone buildings that rose around it.
Surviving ancient literary texts mention a shrine that contained the "House of Romulus," a small hut that the state
maintained and to which Romans came periodically to pay
homage. It was so highly venerated, in fact, that the first em-
peror, Augustus, built his own house nearby, no doubt hoping to promote his image by close identification with the
city's founder. It seems likely that the hut unearthed recently
and the one from the ancient shrine are one and the same.

Also, in 1988 excavators found the remains of a fortification wall, also dating from the eighth century B.C., on the edge of the Palatine. Was this the wall that Romulus built?

At first glance, these discoveries seem to match some of the main points in the founding legend. However, scholars remain skeptical. In the first place, they point out, it is impossible to say when the Romans set up the Romulus shrine. They may have discovered the hut's remains later when digging the foundation of some new building, merely speculated that it was the founder's abode, and on this flimsy basis turned it into a shrine. Even more important, the fact that the huts and wall date from the eighth century B.C. is far from definitive proof that Rome was established at that time. Excavators have determined beyond a doubt that the Palatine and some of the other nearby Roman hills were inhabited long before—at least by 1000 B.C. and likely a good deal earlier. (The evidence consists of graves containing urns filled with the ashes of the cremated inhabitants, in addition to pottery and bronze utensils and other artifacts.)

Regarding the identity and origins of these early inhabitants of the site of Rome, scholars are unsure and somewhat divided. On the one hand, they may have been native to central Italy, an offshoot of what historians term the "Apennine culture," named after the rugged mountain range that runs north-south through the Italian "boot." This Bronze Age society (characterized by the use of tools and weapons made of bronze), which practiced inhumation (burial of the dead), lasted from about 1800 to 1200 B.C. If its members did indeed settle the Roman hills in the second millennium B.C., their society underwent significant changes during the transition from the Bronze Age to the Iron Age (ca. 1200–900 B.C., in which iron tools and weapons came into use). In much of central and northern Italy during these years, population increases occurred, which may have resulted from higher agricultural yields made possible by the spread of more advanced metalworking techniques. Also, the custom of inhumation was largely replaced by cremation. These changes may have been the result of cultural influences filtering in from outside Italy and steadily altering its way of life.

By contrast, a number of historians have long favored another possibility for the origins of the Romans. They propose that the Latin-speaking tribes who gave rise to the Romans migrated into Italy sometime in the second millennium B.C. The traditional view was that they came in waves across the Alps. However, studies of the distribution of early Italian languages have led some scholars to conclude that at least some of them moved southwestward through the Balkans and crossed the Adriatic Sea into eastern Italy. They then migrated a little at a time across the peninsula. One group settled on or near the plain of Latium, and some of its members eventually erected villages on one or more of the Roman hills.

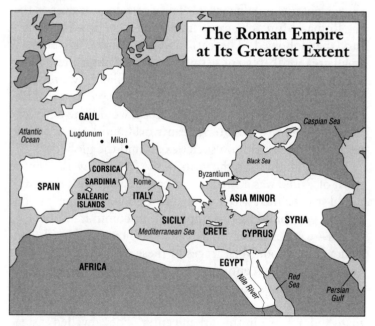

The Roman Monarchy

These questions and theories about primitive Latin/Roman origins aside, it appears that the separate villages on the seven hills came together into a single town in the late eighth century B.C. at the earliest and more credibly in the early to mid–seventh century B.C. It is probably the distant but enduring memory of this event that the later Romans identified with the founding by Romulus. The merger of the villages was, after all, very likely accompanied by much ceremony and the establishment of new and distinct traditions, especially religious ones. Certainly it is very likely that some of Rome's most ancient and venerated religious festivals originated in this period. For example, the Palilia, celebrated on April 21, was designed to protect the community's sheep and cattle as shepherds led them to their summer pastures. And more pointedly, the Septimontium, observed on December 11, commemorated the union of the seven Roman hills and their residents, both previous and present.

Whether the religious union of the villages and their political union were separate events or occurred at the same time is unknown. What seems fairly certain, however, is that the Roman Monarchy came into being sometime in the century that followed. The early kings ruled over a relatively small area, probably consisting of no more than a few dozen square miles, most of it uninhabited farmland, swamps, and forests. At the time, no one could have guessed that this tiny city-state, one among hundreds in Italy, would one day come to rule the entire Mediterranean world and leave a permanent cultural imprint on societies around the globe.

Indeed, all through the years of the Monarchy, the central town of Rome was a small, unimposing place with dirty, unpaved streets lined with huts made of timber and thatch. The few larger buildings—temples and communal meeting places—were smaller than later versions and still constructed of wood. Most traces of these early structures were erased over the centuries that followed as larger, more durable buildings were erected in their places. During the days of the kings and well into republican times, most Romans did not live in this urban center. They dwelled instead in simple huts in the surrounding countryside, hardy shepherds and farmers living a rustic, uncultured existence.

The exact length of the monarchial period, as well as the number of kings and the lengths of their reigns, is unknown. According to later tradition, there were seven kings, beginning with Romulus, who supposedly reigned from 753 to 717 B.C. He was then succeeded by Numa Pompilius, Tullus

Hostilius, Ancus Marcius, Tarquinius Priscus, Servius Tullius, and Tarquinius Superbus (or "Tarquin the Proud"). Some of these rulers, especially the first three, were probably legendary rather than real persons; the last four, however, may well have been real. In any case, recent scholarship suggests that the period of the Monarchy was shorter than traditionally believed. Also, there might have been more than seven kings, some of whose identities and deeds merged with those of the traditional seven in historical accounts fashioned centuries later.

How these rulers were chosen and how much power and authority they held is uncertain. But traditions recorded by Livy and other later writers suggest that some kind of election was held in which selected male citizens, probably those who could afford to bear weapons, met periodically in an assembly and either chose or ratified nominees. More important, those chosen had to be ratified by the heads of the leading families, the so-called Roman fathers (*patres*). They made up a privileged social class—the patricians—who would, as senators and military leaders, exercise profound authority and influence over Roman society for many centuries to come. These fathers granted the assembly "supreme power," Livy wrote, "but on the condition that their election of a king should be valid only if it were ratified by themselves—thus keeping, in effect, as much power as they gave."[10]

Scholars know relatively little about Rome's history during the Monarchy. What is certain is that the Romans were frequently in conflict with their immediate neighbors and that Roman territory steadily expanded outward, especially into the Latium plain in the south. Heroic myths, some of which may be exaggerated versions of real events, tell of Rome's takeover of Alba Longa, the region in which the legendary Aeneas had supposedly settled centuries before. In one of the most famous tales, attributed to the reign of Tullus Hostilius (673–642 B.C.), the Romans and Albans were at war, but they wanted to conserve their manpower to fight their common enemy—the Etruscans. The two sides each chose three champions who would fight to decide the war's outcome. Though two of the three Romans, members of a noble family, the Horatii, were killed, the third was ultimately victorious. "The cheering ranks of the Roman army," Livy recalled, "welcomed back their champion. . . . Alba was subject now to her Roman mistress."[11]

The Etruscans and the Monarchy's Fall

Concerning that common enemy—the Etruscans—the Romans apparently fought them at intervals over a span of several centuries. All the while, especially at times when relations between the two peoples were cordial, the inhabitants of Rome felt the cultural influence of these more advanced neighbors. The Etruscans were an energetic, talented, highly civilized people who lived in well-fortified cities featuring paved streets laid out in logical, convenient grid patterns. Most of what is known about them comes from excavations of their tombs, many of which were discovered in the twentieth century. In one area alone—Tarquinii (a few miles northwest of Rome)—archaeologists found more than five thousand Etruscan tombs in the 1960s. Many of those explored have revealed beautiful wall paintings, sculptures, weapons, pottery, and other grave goods, all providing evidence of a culture that both impressed and inspired the Romans.

Indeed, the Etruscans imparted to the Romans various artistic styles and skills, architectural ideas (such as the arch, which later became a Roman trademark), and certain religious, legal, and political concepts, as well as the "sport" of gladiators fighting to the death. Partly in imitation of Etruscan cities, such as Veii (about ten miles north of Rome), in the late sixth century B.C. Rome began its transformation from a crude, ramshackle town to one with stone sewers, a paved forum (main square), and stone public buildings. The most imposing of these early structures was the first of Rome's temples to its chief god, Jupiter.

The Etruscans may also have had a hand in ending Tarquin's rule and with it the Roman Monarchy. Though a great builder, Tarquin, himself of Etruscan birth, was a tyrant who apparently abused his authority. The actual events of his overthrow and the establishment of the Roman Republic that followed are not well understood. But it seems certain that, as Livy and other later Roman historians claim, the leading patricians had a major hand in ousting him. However, an Etruscan king—Lars Porsenna, of the city of Clusium (about eighty miles northeast of Rome)—may have helped them accomplish this coup. One possible scenario is that Porsenna agreed to aid the rebels in exchange for some favor or other compensation, but then turned on them and occupied the city. (Recent archaeological finds showing that several of Rome's important public buildings burned down about this time may be evidence of a violent takeover.) However, the Romans, with the help of some neighboring Latin cities, soon forced Porsenna to retreat.

The Roman Republic

That left the Romans free to form a new kind of government. Not surprisingly, the Roman fathers rejected the idea of kingship, which they had come to despise, and instead established a republic based on the then-progressive notion of rule by representatives of the people. Roman leaders at first defined "the people" rather narrowly, however. Only free adult males who owned weapons (and were therefore eligible for military service), a group that made up a minority of the population, could vote or hold public office. Some of these citizens met periodically at an assembly, which had more power than its more primitive version in the Monarchy. They proposed and voted on new laws and also annually elected two consuls (administrator-generals) to run the state on a day-to-day basis and to lead the army.

This assembly was in some ways a kind of legislature. Another, more powerful legislative body, the Senate, was composed exclusively of patricians, who held their positions for life. Although in theory the senators were mere governmental advisers, in reality they usually dictated the policies of the consuls and, through the use of wealth and high position, indirectly influenced the way the members of the assembly voted. Thus, except under extreme circumstances, the Senate held the real power in republican Rome; and the state was an oligarchy (a government run by a select group) rather than a true democracy.

Still, in an age when kings and other absolute monarchs ruled almost everywhere else in the known world, the Roman Republic was a very enlightened political entity indeed. Though most Romans did not have a say in state policy, many had a measurable voice in choosing leaders and making laws. And these laws often offered an umbrella of protection against the arbitrary abuses of potentially corrupt leaders to members of all classes. For these and other reasons, republican government proved increasingly flexible and largely met the needs of all Romans.

As a result, the Roman people came to view their system with great pride and patriotism. In time they came to believe that the rise of that system, and indeed the very founding of Rome centuries earlier, was not a chance event; rather, the gods had blessed these national beginnings and ordained that the Romans, the master race, were destined to rule over others. This belief in a greater destiny fueled new and greater stages of Roman expansion. In the late fifth century B.C., Roman armies began marching outward from Latium. They captured the main Etruscan stronghold of Veii in about 396 B.C., and in the decades that followed many other towns and peoples of central Italy became incorporated into the growing Roman sphere. By the early third century, after Rome's defeat of the Samnites, a formidable group of hill tribes, Roman territory had expanded to cover some fifty thousand square miles, more than a hundred times its original size.

Keys to Rome's Success

One important factor in the success of these early conquests was Rome's establishment of "colonies," small towns that served as advanced bases for consolidating recent territorial gains. These colonies were very practical and functional in their layout and demonstrated the Romans' unusual efficiency and practicality. One such base, Alba Fucens (sixty-eight miles east of Rome), set up in 303 B.C. near the end of Rome's second war with the Samnites, was first excavated in 1949. Archaeologists discovered a forum containing a temple, law court, market, baths, and shops.

Another key to the Romans' successful early expansion

was their gift for political conciliation and organization. Only rarely did they treat former enemies harshly, more often choosing the wiser and more fruitful approach of making treaties with them and granting them Roman citizenship and legal privileges. They also initiated the habit of introducing the Latin language, as well as Roman ideas, laws, and customs, to non-Latin peoples, in a sense "Romanizing" them. Noted scholar Michael Grant comments,

> What made the Romans remarkable was a talent for patient political reasonableness that was unique in the ancient world. . . . On the whole, Rome found it advisable . . . to keep its bargains with its allies, displaying a self-restraint, a readiness to compromise, and a calculated generosity that the world had never seen. And so the allies, too, had little temptation to feel misused.[12]

As time went by, more and more of Italy's peoples became such Roman allies or were completely absorbed by Rome. Meanwhile, the Roman appetite for territory and power continued to grow. In the late 280s B.C., Rome turned its attention to the numerous Greek cities that had sprung up across southern Italy in the preceding few centuries. And in the space of only two decades it absorbed them, becoming the undisputed master of all Italy south of the Po Valley (the northern region at the foot of the Alps).

Next, Rome looked beyond the shores of Italy at neighboring Mediterranean coasts. Carthage (centered in what is now Tunisia, in North Africa), fell to Roman steel after the three devastating Punic Wars, fought between 264 and 146 B.C. (The term *Punic*, from the Latin *Punicus*, meaning Carthaginian, came from *Poenus* meaning Phoenician, since the Carthaginians were of Phoeni-

This drawing of a Samnite warrior was copied from an ancient painting.

cian stock.) As prizes, Rome gained the large and fertile island of Sicily at the foot of the Italian boot, other western Mediterranean islands, Spain, and much of North Africa.

Although Rome had long been strictly a land power, out of necessity during the Punic conflicts it built a powerful navy. Soon after obliterating Carthage, it unleashed its formidable combined land and naval forces on the Greek kingdoms clustered in the Mediterranean's eastern sphere, including Macedonia, Seleucia, and Egypt. By the end of the second century B.C., the Mediterranean had become, in effect, a Roman lake. And thereafter, to emphasize that fact, the Romans rather arrogantly referred to the waterway as *mare nostrum,* "our sea."

The rise of Rome from a backward little town on the edge of the known civilized world to the controller of most of that world had taken little more than four centuries. Few other peoples in history, before or after, have enjoyed such unbridled success. And with the exception of the Greeks, no other ancient people went on to influence so many other Western nations with their own customs and ideas. In the modern mind, this series of events was due partly to Roman talent and determination and partly to random chance and just plain good luck. In the Roman mind, however, as Virgil phrased it in the immortal *Aeneid,* it had been fate and the gods, rather than luck, that had guided Rome's course. Virgil's contemporary Livy struck a similar chord when he said, "I must believe that it was already written in the book of fate that this great city of ours should arise, and the first steps be taken to the founding of the mightiest empire the world has known—next to God's."[13] Whether it was fate or chance, what is certain is that the present world would not have become what it is had Rome not risen to help lay its political and cultural foundations.

Notes

1. T.J. Cornell, *The Beginnings of Rome: Italy and Rome from the Bronze Age to the Punic Wars (c. 1000–264 B.C.).* London: Routledge, 1995, p. 4.

2. Cornell, *The Beginnings of Rome,* p. xv.

3. Polybius, *The Histories,* published as *Polybius: The Rise of the Roman Empire.* Trans. Ian Scott-Kilvert. New York: Penguin Books, 1979, p. 41.

4. Varro dated events "from Rome's founding" (*ab urbe condita*, abbreviated AUC). The system that employs the labels B.C. ("before Christ") and A.D. (*"anno Domini,"* meaning "the year of the Lord") was introduced by Christian scholars much later (in the sixth century). These scholars calculated that Christ had been born in the year delineated by Varro as 754 AUC and labeled it A.D. 1 in their new chronology. In their system, therefore, Rome was founded 753 years before the year 1, or 753 B.C.

5. Virgil, *The Aeneid.* Trans. Patric Dickinson. New York: New American Library, 1961, pp. 141–42.

6. Virgil, *The Aeneid*, p. 14.

7. Plutarch, *Life of Romulus*, in *Parallel Lives*, published complete as *Lives of the Noble Grecians and Romans.* Trans. John Dryden. New York: Random House, 1932, p. 31.

8. Livy, *The History of Rome from Its Foundation.* Books 1–5 published as *Livy: The Early History of Rome.* Trans. Aubrey de Sélincourt. New York: Penguin Books, 1971, pp. 40, 42–43.

9. Cornell, *The Beginnings of Rome*, p. 60.

10. Livy, *The History*, in *The Early History of Rome*, p. 52.

11. Livy, *The History*, in *The Early History of Rome*, p. 61.

12. Michael Grant, *History of Rome.* New York: Scribner's, 1978, pp. 55–56.

13. Livy, *The History*, in *The Early History of Rome*, p. 37.

Chapter 1

Rome in Its Infancy

Turning Points

IN WORLD HISTORY

Rome's Geographic Setting

Donald R. Dudley

Much of the personality of the early Romans and their in-
fant city-state was shaped by the nature and setting in
which they and it grew—the climate, terrain, and available
physical resources of western Italy. In this well-informed
examination of that setting, former University of Bir-
mingham scholar Donald R. Dudley begins much later, in
the Augustan Age of the late first century B.C. The writers
of this era, Rome's literary golden age, glowingly described the agrarian beauty and plenty of Roman Italy, and
in this regard Dudley singles out the great Roman poet
Virgil and the Greek historian Dionysius of Halicarnassus. Then Dudley goes on to describe the land, including
the formidable mountain chains, the rich volcanic soils, as
well as some of the early peoples who inhabited the regions surrounding Rome.

The writers of the age of Augustus cherished the belief that
Italy was the most favoured of lands, presenting the opti-
mum conditions for the life of plants, animals and men and
so destined by Nature and the Gods for the seat of a world
Empire. This belief informs the *Georgics* of Virgil and is expressed, in one of his noblest passages, in the Second *Geor-
gic*. In his first book Dionysius of Halicarnassus writes in
more prosaic terms. What he stresses is the range, variety
and high quality of the produce of Italian soil. 'Italy has
plenty of good arable land, but it is not treeless like a mere
grain-bearing country: again, although it produces all kinds
of trees, it does not give a poor corn yield, as does forest
land: yet again, though productive in corn and trees, it is not
unsuitable for ranching: finally, no one can say that, though

rich in corn and cattle and timber, it is unpleasant for men to live in.' He goes on to justify Italy's claim to all-round excellence. 'What corn lands can compare with the plains of Campani, which yield three crops a year? What olives excel those of Messapia and many another district? What vines the Tuscan and Alban and Falernian? There are good pastures for sheep and goats, wonderful grazing for horses and cattle, in the water meadows and the mountain glens. The forest resources of Italy are the most wonderful of all—the Sila and the Monte Gargano and those of Alpine lands—giving first quality timber for shipbuilding, houses and all other purposes. Add to these hotsprings, minerals, wild game and abundance of fish and above all a temperate climate, never by excessive cold or heat harmful to growing crops or animals. In short Italy excels any other land in general fertility and all-round usefulness.' I have quoted this passage at length because it is the most explicit statement of the advantages of living in Italy, but it could be supported by many a passage from [the works of the Greek and Roman writers] Strabo, Varro, Columella and Pliny.

Formidable Mountain Barriers

Behind these Augustan and later writers lay a thousand years and more of hard work on the land of Italy. The modern geographer is likely to provide a cooler appraisal. The long peninsula of Italy juts out more than 700 miles to the southeast from the main land mass of Europe. The great arc of the Alps seems to provide a natural frontier on the north, with a wide barrier of mountain land. This high mountainwall is most formidable in its western sectors, where mountains of 12–15,000 feet and high passes cut off Italy from Switzerland and France. Even the coast provides no easy passage. The train between Genoa and Marseilles keeps diving into tunnels; the motorist on the Corniche road above finds it impossible to overtake heavy trucks on the incessant bends. But on the north-east the Carnic and Julian Alps provide a series of easier passes—the Brenner, the Plöcken and the Pear Tree Pass—leading into the Danube Valley, the great artery of communication in prehistoric Europe. These are the routes by which the earliest land immigrants from continental Europe came to the Po Valley and on into peninsular Italy. When Virgil calls the Po the king of rivers we hear the voice of a man who had spent his childhood in Cisalpine Gaul and who saw no river so majestic when he moved south to Rome and Campania. Swollen by the melting snows from the Alps, the Po and its tributaries provided a primitive landscape of marsh, scrub, and forest, with relatively few patches of drier ground.

Invading peoples who found their way to the crossings of the Po would see before them to the south another mountain barrier. The Apennines, beginning at the Gulf of Genoa, provide the broad backbone of peninsular Italy and are protracted so far as the toe of Italy, falling just short of a physical link with the high mountains of eastern Sicily. The Apennine summits mostly run between four and five thousand feet, though there is a patch of high mountain country in the Abruzzi, where the Gran Sasso d'Italia reaches 9,850 feet. The summits do not rise from a main chain; there is instead a complex deeply dissected mountain system, enclosing many deep glens and flanked by outlying ranges on either side. The passes across these mountains are difficult but far from impossible, though the winters are surprisingly hard. They foster isolated pastoral communities, whose economy has lasted down to our own time. They make Italy a Janus-like land, facing in opposite directions. [This is a reference to the Roman god Janus, who had two faces.] Its western coasts, washed by the Tyrrhenian Sea, look to communications with France, Spain and North Africa. The east and south-east coasts look across the stormy Adriatic to the treacherous, mountainous shores of Dalmatia and Epirus, to Greece and to the sea routes which lead into the Aegean. Neither coastline of Italy is blessed with good harbours. The Gulf of Otranto, the Bay of Naples and Genoa provide good harbours for modern liners; on the Adriatic side incessant labour is required to keep the port of Venice in operation and the city itself above the waves. Ancient ships could of course make use of much smaller ports, but only provided they could find sheltered anchorage.

Rich Volcanic Soils

On the western side of the Apennines—very much the more
attractive—peninsular Italy has three notable areas of good
soil—Tuscany, Latium and Campania. All three possess volcanic soils of exceptional fertility and in early times offered
by far the most favourable prospects for settlement. They
also posed a perpetual challenge to the pastoralists who
looked down on them from their high grazing grounds in
the Apennines. They needed these lowland pastures for their
winter grazing and even when the drovers' ways and drovers'
rights had been established by legislation, the passage of
their flocks provided many disputes between them and the
men of the plains. The Adriatic coast lacks such sharply dif-
ferentiated lands as Latium and Campania. Instead, a long
coastal strip extends from Ancona to Foggia, with the isolated peninsula of Monte Gargano as an outlier of the Apennines. This is the land known to the Romans as Picenum and
its cultural history in early times is not very well understood.
Beyond it the limestone grazing lands of Apulia and Calabria
extend to the heel of Italy. This again is pastoral country, its
low rainfall restricting the growth of agriculture.

Early Italian Peoples

In about 850 B.C., when our story begins, Italy was something of a cultural backwater. No ancient civilisation had appeared on her soil comparable to those of Crete or Myce-
naean Greece, let alone the great civilisations of the Near
East. Not that she altogether lacked contact with the higher
cultures of the Aegean. Indeed a memory of such contacts is
preserved in the legends of the voyages of Odysseus and of
the Argonauts, the coming of Aeneas to Italy and even the
flight of Daedalus. Archaeology can point to evidence of a
trade with the Aegean. There may have been in Minoan
times trading posts on Italian soil, the forerunners of the
later Greek colonies. But this was trade, not settlement—except perhaps at Cumae. There is no evidence that any of the
early cultures of Italy were able to produce anything so complex, from a technological point of view, as Stonehenge or
Avebury in remote Britain. The culture of Bronze Age Sar-

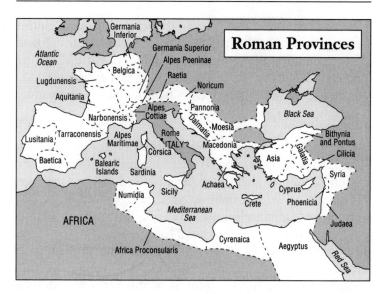

Roman Provinces

Germania Inferior
Germania Superior
Alpes Poeninae
Atlantic Ocean
Belgica
Lugdunensis
Raetia
Aquitania
Noricum
Alpes Cottiae
Pannonia
Narbonensis
Dalmatia
Moesia
Black Sea
Lusitania
Tarraconensis
Alpes Maritimae
Rome
ITALY
Macedonia
Bithynia and Pontus
Baetica
Corsica
Galatia
Cilicia
Balearic Islands
Sardinia
Asia
Syria
Numidia
Sicily
Achaea
Cyprus
Crete
Phoenicia
AFRICA
Mediterranean Sea
Judaea
Africa Proconsularis
Cyrenaica
Aegyptus
Red Sea

dinia, with its . . . sculptures in stone and bronze, represents the most advanced society known in Italian lands during the second millennium B.C.

The Ligurians of the Maritime Alps were one of the earliest of all Italian peoples. This ancient race, perhaps of Sicilian or North African origin, also inhabited the islands of Sardinia and Elba. They survived many centuries in their mountains before they were overrun by the Romans. In the north-east another ancient people, the Veneti, perhaps of Illyrian origin, occupied the lands which still bear their name. We know little about the peoples who in 850 B.C. inhabited what is now Lombardy and Piedmont—for this is before the Etruscans or the Celts had penetrated those lands. In the light of its later history, the most important peoples in Italy were those kindred stocks who had already settled themselves in the highland pastures of the Apennines as far down as the mountains that bound Campania and who were disputing possession of the western plains with their earliest inhabitants. These peoples—the Umbrians, the Sabines, the Marsi, the Samnites, the Latins and a large number of smaller communities into which they were divided, appear repeatedly in Roman history. Their languages were closely related and two of them, Oscan and Latin, would obtain wide currency. These were the people who, from

Latium northwards, had reached the level of material culture best represented by the famous site of Villanova, near Bologna. The exploitation of the mineral resources of Etruria, and especially the use of iron, had produced in this district the most advanced culture yet to be seen in Italy. Latium was very much a backward area, compared with the north.

The Map of Italy Still Incomplete

The land of Italy around 850 B.C. is thus one of little local cultures, none of them very far advanced. Many languages are spoken in it, and there is no kind of ethnic unity. The very name is an anachronism. There is no common term as yet for the peninsula as a whole. Complex as it is, the ethnic and linguistic map of Italy is still incomplete. Three important elements have yet to be added to it. During the eighth century B.C., the higher cultures of the Etruscans and the Greeks will be introduced. About two centuries later a new wave of invading peoples will bring the Celts from the Upper Danube into the valley of the Po. [And eventually the Romans will emerge from their obscurity to dominate all of these peoples.]

Rome's Legendary Founding

Antony Kamm

The actual founding of Rome, the so-called "eternal city," is shrouded forever in the mists of time and cannot be completely separated from the popular legends that later grew up about it. In this essay, Antony Kamm, of England's University of Stirling, summarizes the legendary founding, in which the key characters were the Trojan prince Aeneas and the Italian hero Romulus. Kamm then proceeds to tell what scholars know about the actual founding, in the process describing the site of Rome and the early Latin tribes that settled there.

The Romans themselves were in no doubt when Rome was founded: 21 April 753 BC. On that day of the year, too, they celebrated the traditional festival of the Parilia in honour of Pales, the god (or goddess—the Romans were notoriously vague about the gender of some of their deities) of shepherds and sheep. In 1948 traces were found on the Palatine Hill, the central and most easily fortified of the seven hills of the ultimate city, of the huts of a settlement of shepherd folk dating from about 750 BC. Current excavations have uncovered the remains of a ritual boundary wall of about the same period.

The Romulus Legend

The legend of the founding of Rome by Romulus was circulating 400 years later at the most. It tells how a local king, Numitor of Alba Longa, was ejected by his younger brother, Amulius. To secure his position, Amulius then murdered Numitor's sons and forced Numitor's daughter, Rhea Silvia, to become a vestal virgin, thus, he thought, preventing her from having any children, at least for the time being. Vestal virgins normally served as priestesses in the temple of Vesta for thirty years from between 6 and 10 years old, and the penalty for failing to remain virginal was a singularly nasty death. Rhea Silvia, however, caught the lascivious eye of the god Mars, who had his way with her while she slept. The outcome of this unconscious but divine experience was twin sons, who were named Romulus and Remus.

There was a fine rumpus. Amulius had Rhea Silvia thrown into the river Tiber, where she sank conveniently into the arms of the god of the river, who married her. The twins were also consigned to the Tiber, but in a reed basket, which floated away until it was caught in the branches of a fig tree. They were suckled by a she-wolf (appropriately, for wolves were sacred to Mars) until the royal shepherd found them and rescued them. In another version of the story they were breast-fed by this wife, a former prostitute, who had just lost a stillborn child—the Latin word *lupa* means both 'she-wolf' and 'prostitute'.

The couple cared for Romulus and Remus and in due course revealed to them the circumstances of their birth. Amulius was killed in battle and their grandfather Numitor was restored to his throne. As a contribution to the ensuing celebrations, the brothers resolved to establish a new city near the spot where they had been washed ashore. They took omens by watching the flight of birds, which indicated that the city should be built on the Palatine Hill, on which Romulus was standing, and that he should be its king. Romulus then set about marking the boundary with a plough drawn by a white cow and a white bull. Remus, either in fun or as a gesture of derision, committed the impropriety of jumping over the furrow. Romulus lost his temper and killed his twin.

The embryo city, still no more than a settlement, was rather short of women. Romulus invited the neighbouring Sabine tribe to a programme of games he was organizing to mark the harvest festival. When the guests were comfortably settled, the Romans, as they were now known, abducted at swordpoint 600 Sabine daughters, all but one of them, it is said, virgins. In an addition to the traditional story, they proved to be sterile until Juno, goddess, among other things, of childbirth, took a hand and sorted out the problem. Or it may be that the Sabine women, having suffered abduction, refused at first to co-operate with their self-styled husbands.

Aeneas: Father of the Roman Race?

A further tradition, well known at least by 240 BC, traces the origins of Rome to the even earlier time of the legendary Trojan hero, Aeneas, son of a mortal father and of the goddess Venus. He fought against the Greeks in the Trojan War, escaped from the sack of the city, and, after many wanderings, changes in fortune, and divine interventions, landed in Italy and founded the dynasty from which Romulus eventually came. This was the version of the story much favoured by the emperors of Rome, who liked to think of themselves as being nominally descended from the ancient heroes, and by the Romans themselves, who could thus see the early history of their city, which was one of continual struggle for survival, reflected in heroic legend. It was written up in verse by Virgil (70–19 BC), largely in response to the encouragement of [the emperor] Augustus, in the *Aeneid*, which was published posthumously. It is the national epic of the Roman Empire, and the most famous poem of the Roman era.

According to the legend, and to Virgil, Aeneas cast anchor at the mouth of the Tiber.

> Now, Aeneas, looking out from the glassy ocean, sees a vast stretch of forest. The river Tiber's pleasant stream flows through it before bursting into the sea in swirling eddies made yellow by the copious sandy sediment. Above and all around, different kinds of birds indigenous to the river banks and reaches sweeten the air with song as they dart among the trees. Having ordered his companions to change course and steer for land, Aeneas is elated as he makes the river's shade.
>
> (*Aeneid*, VII. 29–36)

The Tiber flowed through Latium, whose king, Latinus, had had divine intimation that he should hand over his daughter in marriage to a stranger. So he offers her to Aeneas, much to the discomfort of another local king, Turnus of the Rutuli, who fancies her for himself. Reluctantly drawn into war, Aeneas obtains the support of Tarchon, king of the Etruscans, and finally triumphs.

The Town's Early Growth

In this excerpt from his widely read study of twentieth-century archaeology in Italy, The Mute Stones Speak, *scholar Paul MacKendrick briefly describes how the original Roman settlements consisted of simple huts and how a more formal, developed town slowly grew.*

What later was unified into urban Rome was originally a group of simple hut-villages clustered on various hills, the Forum huts having spilled down, as it were, from the village on the Palatine. The huts in the level just above the Forum necropolis represent a still earlier stage of this spillover.... By the date of ... [the] earliest pebble pavements, the huts in the necropolis area have been replaced by a more developed domestic architecture, perhaps with rooms opening on a central court. These houses have rectangular plans, mud-brick, wood-braced walls, and tufa foundations. At the spillover stage, the villagers from the various hills formed some kind of confederation symbolized archaeologically by the two types of graves in the Forum necropolis, and in literature by the tradition of the joint religious festival called the Septimontium.

The period of the first pebble pavement (575 B.C.) is one of major change, from village to urban life, to a city now for the first time boasting a civic center, destined to become the world's most famous public square, the Roman Forum. Of the same date are the earliest remains on the Capitoline Hill, which was to be the *arx* or citadel of historic Rome. Of the same date are the earliest artifacts from the Regia, which later generations revered as the palace of the kings. Of the same date is a sophisticated phase of the round shrine of Vesta [goddess of the hearth], which encircled the sacred flame, symbol of the city's continuity.

Paul MacKendrick, *The Mute Stones Speak: The Story of Archaeology in Italy.* New York: St. Martin's Press, 1960, p. 73.

The historical sack of Troy was in about 1220 BC. To cover the period between the presumed arrival of Aeneas and the traditional date for the founding of Rome, the Romans invented a string of monarchs from Ascanius, son of Aeneas by his first (Trojan) wife, to Numitor. Though there is no firm tradition about Aeneas's death, there is an intriguing reference to a tomb in the Greek historian, Dionysius of Halicarnassus, who lived in Rome at the very end of the first century BC.

> The Latins built a hero-shrine to Aeneas, inscribing it to him as 'The god and father of this place, who guides the waters of the Numicius [a river in Latium]'. . . . It is an earth mound, not very big, with trees set around it in regular rows well worth seeing.
>
> (*Roman Antiquities*, I. 64)

The shrine that Dionysius visited at Lavinium is almost certainly the seventh-century BC tumulus excavated in 1968. Originally it contained a burial chest, which was rifled about a hundred years later. The tomb was restored at the end of the fourth century BC.

The Historical Founding by the Latins

So much for the legend. Historically, Latium and Etruria (land of the Etruscans) were crucial in the development of Rome into 'an autonomous and then an independent city state, though it is not known for certain where the original Latins and Etruscans came from. The Latins who first settled on the Palatine Hill, however, had been in the region since about 1000 BC. They herded sheep, goats, and cattle, and kept pigs. In the manner of such people, they lived in small scattered communities, in round or oblong huts made of wooden poles interwoven with twigs and branches and then covered with clay.

The summit of the hill itself was roughly trapezoidal in shape, the longest side being about 400 metres long. On three sides, the rock sloped steeply down into valleys which were often full of flood water. On the other, north-eastern, side, a narrow saddle of rock led to the adjoining hill. The cluster of hills, each between 60 and 100 metres high, stood on a plateau above the surrounding plain, the soil of which was continually enriched by deposits of volcanic silt from the Tiber and its tributaries. We may imagine, then, the summit of the Palatine Hill covered with clusters of small thatched huts of wood and clay, and somewhere a flat, open meeting space, the forerunner of the Roman forum. The burial place was in the marshy ground at the foot of the hill, where years later would stand the great forum of republican and imperial Rome. Only infants, and sometimes young children, appear to have been buried within the community.

The site was an inspired one for other reasons, too. The sea, with its potential for foreign trade, was only a few kilometres downstream. The hill overlooked the shallows which constituted the most convenient point for crossing the river as it neared the sea, and thus commanded the main route along western Italy. The city lay mid-way between the north and south of Italy, that natural formation of land enclosed by the Alps to the north, and by the sea everywhere else. Furthermore, Italy itself lay centrally in the Mediterranean, with ready access to the rest of Europe, to Africa, and to the east. Thus the fourteenth-century proverb, 'All roads lead to Rome', was true from the start.

Rome's Early Neighbors

Michael Crawford

Because the Romans readily absorbed some of the customs and ideas of the neighboring peoples they encountered, traded with, fought, and eventually conquered, it is essential to understand who some of Rome's early neighbors were and how they contributed to the ongoing expansion and cultural development of the Roman city-state. Here, Michael Crawford, of University College, London, a noted scholar of Roman civilization, examines the three peoples who affected the Romans the most in their early years—the hill tribes of the Apennines, especially the Samnites, who fought a number of bloody wars with the Romans; the Greeks, who settled many sites in southern Italy; and the Etruscans, who lived in Etruria, the region lying just north of Rome.

It is important to have some understanding of the diverse elements which comprise the mixture which we call Roman Italy; this not only because these various elements each influenced Rome in the period when Rome was still a small city state, but also because all of them directly affected the nature of the eventual mixture.

It is for these reasons as well as because of the distinctive nature of certain Roman institutions that if any other power had united Italy the result would have been different; though, it must be said, the view that if the Samnites, for instance, had united Italy the result would have been federation rather than domination is merely the transposition to the ancient world of modern wishful thinking.

The three main groups involved are the people of the central Italian highlands, culturally on a level with or inferior to the Romans, but ethnically related and using a variety of Italic languages related to Latin; the Greeks of the south Italian colonies; and the Etruscans. These two were both culturally more advanced than Rome, but in varying degrees alien in race and language. The Gauls of the Po valley, culturally no more advanced than the Romans and of alien race and language were in due course in effect exterminated and their culture destroyed.

There is a further reason for spending some time on the non-Roman peoples of Italy. The Etruscans, to a certain extent, and the Greeks of the south to a much greater extent, both of them in contact with other areas of the Mediterranean world, provided for the expanding [Roman state] avenues leading to involvement with that world.

The Hill Peoples

The peoples of the central Italian highlands survive in the literary record chiefly as bitter and often successful opponents of the extension of Roman control; the most prominent group, the Samnites . . . lived, as recent archaeological work shows, in settled farmsteads, cultivating cereals as well as olives and vines; for despite their height and relative inaccessibility the Appennines include numerous pockets of agricultural land; the Samnites had few cattle, but many pigs and large flocks of sheep and goats, which were no doubt moved over short distances between summer pastures and winter pastures close to the farmsteads (a technique known as transhumance); both sheep and goats provided milk for cheese, wool, and whey for pig-food, as well as meat when killed at a ripe old age. The symbiotic relationship between plain and hill which transhumance involved was clearly widespread in Appennine Italy and no doubt supported a basically similar economy throughout.

Spreading outwards from the hills, partly by way of raids, but eventually with more serious intent, the peoples of the central Italian highlands were attracted by the fertile plains of Campania, just as the Volscians farther north were attracted by the plains of Latium; the Etruscan city of Capua fell in 423, the Greek city of Cumae in 421, a Greek element in the population surviving in the case of the latter. Neapolis (Naples) remained the only Greek city in Campania, though even there infiltration took place; the Greek cities of the south came similarly under pressure from the tribes of the hinterland. In the end, the hills were conquered by the plains, but at the turn of the fifth and fourth centuries BC it was by no means an obvious outcome.

Greeks in Italy

Of the three groups of people whom I wish to discuss, the Greeks are on the whole the most straightforward. A variety of Greek cities had planted a string of self-governing founda- tions along the coasts of Italy and Sicily, beginning with Pithe- cusae (Ischia) about 775 [BC]; the earliest of these colonies, as they are rather inappropriately described, was almost certainly intended to act as an entrepôt for trade with Etruria; but its own foundation on the mainland opposite, Cumae, was an agricultural community, as were the vast majority of Greek colonies both in the west and elsewhere.

Greek colonization, invariably the venture of an organized community, involved the transfer of a developed society and culture, of its political organization, religious organization, language, monetary system; the colonial experience and con- tact with indigenous populations might eventually lead of course to considerable transformations.

But Magna Graecia, the collective name for the Greek cities in Italy and Sicily, was very much part of the Greek world. . . . Men from the west participated in the great Greek festivals and their successes were celebrated by the Greek poet Pindar in the fifth century BC. In the fourth cen- tury Timoleon of Corinth set out to rescue Sicily from Carthage and . . . a succession of Greek condottieri [leaders of bands of mercenary soldiers] attempted to help Tarentum (Taranto) in her wars with the tribes of the hinterland. The last of them, Pyrrhus of Epirus, fought a full-scale war against Rome, by then the major threat. . . .

The Etruscans

The Etruscans are *sui generis* [unique] and were so regarded in classical antiquity; it was a unique characteristic of their religion that it was centred on sacred writings that had supposedly emanated from supernatural sources, and they also claimed a special ability to discover the will of the gods by a variety of processes of divination [interpreting supposed divine signs in nature]. Furthermore, Etruscan society was characterized, at any rate in its upper echelons, by the relatively high status of its female members and, as a whole, by a deep division between the governing class and a serf population.

Etruscan culture evolved from the Villanovan culture of

The Etruscan City-States

In this tract from his general history of Rome, noted classical scholar Michael Grant provides much useful information about the Etruscan city-states, especially those in closest proximity to Rome, which exerted a strong cultural influence on the emerging Romans.

The Etruscans owed to their eastern forebears, as well as to the Greeks when they subsequently got to know them, a marked talent for urbanization, and this was encouraged by the compulsion, imposed by Italy's geography, to cluster together on the relatively few sites that were eligible and attractive. And so the Etruscans created their cities, first near the coast, and then on inland sites towards the middle course of the Tiber. Traditionally there were twelve such communities in Etruria, though it is hard to draw up a complete list for any given time, and archaeology has revealed a number of townships far exceeding that total. But twelve was the approximate number of their major city-states.

In spite of traditions that there had once been a single king over the whole country, each of these cities seems to have been fully independent of all the rest. Once a year (at least in later times) they sent delegates over their excellent roads to a joint gathering at the shrine of the divinity Voltumna, which has not yet been identified but was probably not far from Lake Volsiniensis (Bolsena). Yet the political initiatives that this loose cult union attempted were apparently rare and generally ineffectual. True, its member cities no doubt maintained shifting patterns of alliances with one another. But they had grown up central Italy and was from the eighth century BC onwards both extraordinarily receptive of foreign influences and extraordinarily adept at integrating them in a local framework. The Etruscans borrowed most perhaps from the Greeks, from whom they imported on an enormous scale fine pottery in exchange for metal; the origin of their language is mysterious.

By the end of the eighth century BC they occupied the area bounded by the River Arno, the Appennines, the Tiber and the sea; during the sixth and fifth centuries they estab-

in physical isolation, kept apart by the wooded and hilly country that surrounded them. In consequence, each city usually tended to act on its own.

And indeed these states were not only independent but also highly individual and distinguished from each other by sharp political, social, and cultural differences—almost as great perhaps as those that distinguished, say, Athens, Corinth, and Sparta in Greece. This point, too rarely appreciated, is of major importance to early Roman history, for Rome was influenced at most significant junctures not by the Etruscans as a whole, but by this or that Etruscan city-state. Owing to the inadequate state of our sources, we cannot always say which of these cities exercised such effect at any given moment. But obviously, to a large extent Rome is likely to have been most greatly influenced by the southern communities, which lay so close to the Tiber. They were Tarquinii (Tarquinia), Caere (Cerveteri), and Veii (Veio), only forty, twenty, and twelve miles distant respectively from Rome. These south Etruscan cities, standing on their hilltops in close proximity to the coast, were livelier and more cosmopolitan, more open and receptive to Greek and other foreign contacts than their middle and north Etruscan counterparts, which lay beyond almost untouched forests in the interior. And so it was they, Tarquinii, Caere, and Veii, that developed a particularly brilliant and prosperous culture in ca. 670–630 B.C. and supplied the formative stimulus and inspiration that transformed Rome from a huddle of hut villages into a city.

Michael Grant, *History of Rome*. New York: Scribner's, 1978, pp. 14–15.

lished an empire in Campania, probably beginning at the coast and in due course occupying Capua. . . . During the fifth and fourth centuries they created another empire in the Po valley; as a by-product of this process of expansion, Rome was ruled for a time by kings who were in effect Etruscan condottieri. The process of expansion was not a single national effort, but reflected the disunity of Etruria and its division into independent city units.

The Etruscans provided Rome with early access to at any rate a form of Greek culture; they also probably provided Rome with some of her insignia of office. . . . More fundamentally, the Capitoline Triad [Rome's group of three major gods] of Jupiter, Juno and Minerva is of Etruscan origin. . . .

The Etruscan empire in Campania was destroyed by the Samnites, the empire in the Po valley by the Gauls. Etruria itself was progressively subjugated by Rome, much aided by the fragility of Etruscan social structures. . . . [Like the central hill tribes and Italian Greeks, therefore, the Etruscans might have come to control much or even all of Italy had it not been for the rise of the aggressive and highly successful Roman city-state.]

Kings and Kingmakers of the Roman Monarchy

T.J. Cornell

In this excerpt from his informative book, *The Beginnings of Rome*, noted scholar T.J. Cornell begins by summarizing the legends of Rome's traditional seven kings and their deeds. Then he examines the era of the Roman Monarchy (which he refers to as the regal period) and concludes that it was probably shorter than as portrayed by tradition. Finally, Cornell deals in some detail with the status of the kings within the state and the method in which they were chosen. He makes the point that the Roman nobles, the wealthy landowners called patricians, likely played a crucial role in this process.

Early Rome was ruled by kings. Of that there can be no doubt. But when it comes to reconstructing the history of the regal period, all we can be certain of is that much of our information is legendary. Traditionally there were seven kings, some of whom are probably historical, at least in the sense that men named Numa Pompilius, Tullus Hostilius, and so on, may indeed have ruled at Rome. But that does not take us very far (and is not certain in any case). Paradoxically, some of the actions for which they were supposedly responsible are more easily authenticated than the kings themselves. For example, although Romulus is legendary, institutions attributed to him can be shown to be historical and to date back to the early regal period. This is simply another way of saying that information about institutions and structures is more reliable than that dealing with individual persons and events. . . .

Excerpted from *The Beginnings of Rome: Italy and Rome from the Bronze Age to the Punic Wars (c 1000–264 B.C.)*, by T.J. Cornell (London: Routledge). Copyright © 1995 T.J. Cornell. Reprinted by permission of Taylor & Francis Books Ltd.

The Traditional Seven Kings

It is clear enough that the earliest kings of Rome are mythical or semi-mythical persons. The first king, Romulus (tradition-ally 753–717 BC), probably never existed. His name appears to be a crude eponym formed from the name of the city; it has the form of an adjective, and means simply 'Roman'. His biogra-phy is a complex mixture of legend and folk-tale, interspersed with antiquarian speculation and political propaganda. . . .

The successors of Romulus, Numa Pompilius (716–674 BC) and Tullus Hostilius (673–642 BC), are little more than contrasting stereotypes, the one pacific and devout, the other warlike and ferocious. These two may conceivably be historical, although the surviving accounts of their reigns are a mixture of legend and conscious antiquarian reconstruc-tion. Tradition credited Numa with all the major religious institutions of the state, including the calendar and the priesthoods. The central episode in the saga of Tullus Hos-tilius was the war against Alba Longa. This war provided the setting for the legend of Horatius, one of the most famous of all Roman stories. Horatius was the victorious survivor of the battle between the Horatii and the Curiatii, two sets of triplets who fought as champions on behalf of Rome and Alba Longa. . . . On his triumphant return to the city, Hor-atius was met at the gate by his sister, who had been be-trothed to one of the Curiatii. When she shed tears on learn-ing of their fate, Horatius killed her in a fit of rage. The war itself, which led to the conquest of Alba Longa and its terri-tory, is historical in the sense that the region of the Alban Hills became part of Roman territory at some point in the regal period. For all we know, this could have been accom-plished by a king named Tullus Hostilius.

The fourth and fifth kings, Ancus Marcius (641–617 BC) and L. Tarquinius Priscus (616–578 BC), are more rounded, and perhaps more historical, figures than their predecessors. Ancus was of Sabine origin, and a grandson (on his mother's side) of Numa. He was celebrated by tradition for building the first bridge across the Tiber (the Pons Sublicius), for ex-tending Roman territory as far as the coast and for the foun-dation of Ostia at the mouth of the river. The Romans of later times remembered him as a popular and beneficent ruler. . . . His successor, L. Tarquinius Priscus, was of part-Etruscan origin, and enjoyed a successful reign as a warrior, constitutional innovator and civic benefactor. He increased the size of the Senate and the cavalry, and instituted games and public entertainments. . . .

The sixth king, Servius Tullius (578–534 BC), is the most complex and enigmatic of them all. The widely differing accounts of his origins and background—in short, of who he was—form only one part of the puzzle. The manner in which he obtained the throne, and the nature of the far-reaching reforms he then instituted, are equally problematic. There is no doubt, however, that the achievements attributed to him—the reorganisation of the citizen body, the construction of temples, public buildings and fortifications, and important initiatives in international affairs—have a firm historical basis and can in some cases be directly confirmed by independent evidence. Another point is that the nature of the kingship changed under Servius Tullius, who did not (unlike his predecessors) obtain the throne in a regular manner, but relied on popular support and became not so much a king as a kind of proto-republican magistrate.

The last king, L. Tarquinius Superbus (Tarquin the Proud, 534–509 BC), was a tyrant pure and simple. The son of the elder Tarquin, he seized the throne by force after murdering his father-in-law Servius. He was cruel and capricious, but also flamboyant and successful. Under his rule, Rome became the dominant power in central Italy, and its prosperity was reflected in the monumental development of the city. The crowning achievement of Tarquin's reign was the construction of the great temple of Capitoline Jupiter, one of the largest and most impressive structures in the Mediterranean world at that time. Just as the temple was completed, but before he had a chance to dedicate it, Tarquin was expelled from the city by a group of aristocrats who set up a republic in his place.

Too Few Kings or Too Many Years?

The first step in any attempt to check the historical credentials of the traditional narrative must be to compare it with the archaeological record. In doing so one is immediately struck by an apparent discrepancy in the chronology. Tradition makes the regal period last for nearly two and a half centuries, stretching back from the fall of Tarquin to the foundation of the city in 754/3 BC. But . . . the archaeological evidence suggests that the formation of the city-state occurred in the later part of the seventh century. There are two ways of resolving this difficulty. The first is to shorten the reigns of the kings, and to suppose that they ruled for around 120 years altogether instead of 240. The alternative is to retain the traditional chronology and to split the regal period in half: on this view the earlier kings would belong to the pre-urban phase, and the dramatic transformation of the community in the later seventh century would coincide with the arrival of the Tarquins.

Perhaps surprisingly, the majority of modern experts opt for the second of these alternatives. Almost all recent accounts of early Rome either state or imply (or take it for granted) that the accession of Tarquinius Priscus coincided with a major break in the historical development of regal Rome. I say surprisingly because no such break is recorded in the sources (although scholars frequently assert the contrary), and because if one thing is certain about the regal period, it is that the traditional chronology is historically impossible. It seems hardly necessary to state that an aggregate of 244 years for seven kings is without historical parallel and cannot be taken seriously.

On any rational view the Roman king-list must be adjusted in one of two ways. Either we must suppose that there were more than seven kings, or we must shorten the chronology. Indeed there are good reasons for doing both as we shall see, the canonical list of seven kings is almost certainly incomplete and the simplest way to resolve the conflict between the tradition and the archaeological record is to date all the historical developments of the regal period, including the kings themselves (if they are authentic), in the period between *c.* 625 and *c.* 500 BC.

But this revision goes against the prevailing current of modern scholarly opinion, which inclines to accept the traditional chronology, and to assume that the accession of Tarquinius Priscus marked an important turning-point in the history of the regal period. This notion needs further discussion, and the contrary view being presented here requires a detailed defence. In modern studies the rise of the Tarquin dynasty is presented in a number of different ways. Some experts regard it as the beginning of the historical age of Rome, and consign the earlier period to legend. Others stress the primitive character of the preceding phase, and contrast it with the prosperous and sophisticated urban culture introduced by the Tarquins. . . . A third strand in contemporary scholarship places heavy emphasis on ethnicity: on this view the accession of Tarquinius Priscus represents the end of a 'Latino-Sabine' period, and the start of an Etruscan phase.

These three ways of defining the issue are not mutually exclusive; on the contrary, they are frequently combined, and most modern accounts contain aspects of all three. It is widely believed that the Tarquins ushered in a period of Etruscan rule, and that for a time Rome became an 'Etruscan city'. On this view it was the Etruscans who were responsible for all the political, economic and cultural changes that Rome underwent during the last century of the monarchy; it was the Etruscans, in short, who made Rome into a city. This Etruscan hypothesis . . . in the opinion of the present writer, however . . . has no warrant either in the written sources or in the archaeological record, and is one of the most pernicious errors currently obscuring the study of archaic Rome. . . .

Relations Among the Monarchs

We may conclude . . . with a few remarks on the nature of Roman kingship, as it is represented in the sources, and on the changes that occurred in the last decades of the monarchic period. The most obvious peculiarity about the Roman kingship is that it was not hereditary. In the developed legend of the origins of Rome, the son of Aeneas founded a hereditary dynasty at Alba Longa. But this Alban dynasty was an antiquarian fiction devised for chronographic reasons; the reality of Roman kingship (and perhaps of kingship in other Italian city-states) was different. No king of Rome inherited the throne from his father; the only partial exception is the last king, Tarquin the Proud, who was the son of the elder Tarquin. But Tarquin's reign did not follow on directly from that of his father; and since he was by all accounts a usurper who seized the throne illegally, it is an exception that proves the rule, and indeed confirms that in normal circumstances hereditary succession was excluded.

According to the received tradition, the rule was observed even in the case of kings who were survived by legitimate sons. The clearest instance of this is the accession of Tarquin the Elder, who was chosen as king even though his predecessor, Ancus Marcius, had left two grown-up sons. The story is complicated, however, by the fact that Tarquin is said to have arranged for the sons of Ancus Marcius to be sent away from Rome a few days before the election of a new king. The Marcii were also supposedly responsible for the murder of Tarquin himself; but . . . this mysterious tale is rather nonsensical, since the assassination produced the very result the Marcii had set out to prevent, namely the accession of Servius Tullius as Tarquin's successor. . . .

How these elements of the traditional account are to be explained is open to debate. The most probable interpretation would seem to be that the Roman monarchy was an elective system, but one in which connections, sometimes blood relationships, existed between some of the kings and their successors. We are given to understand, for instance, that kings were able to designate their chosen successors by giving them positions of responsibility; thus Tarquinius Priscus was the 'right-hand man' of his predecessor Ancus Marcius, and was succeeded in his turn by his own favourite, Servius Tullius.

A further sign of this connection between kings and their successors is that they were frequently related by marriage. Servius Tullius was the son-in-law of Tarquinius Priscus, and Tarquinius Superbus was the son-in-law of Servius Tullius. There is a folk-tale element in such stories: an outsider marries the king's daughter and thereby obtains the kingdom. A classic instance of this motif is the story of Aeneas, who married Lavinia, daughter of King Latinus, and on his death became the ruler of the Latins. In general the process means no more than that the most evident way a king can show favour to a would-be successor is to offer him his daughter's hand. This is more probable than the suggestion that in Rome the succession 'passed through the female line'. Nevertheless, it is undeniable that in the story of the Roman monarchy women are sometimes instrumental in the process of succession, and play an important king-making role. . . .

An important feature of Roman monarchy is that many kings were outsiders—literally so in the cases of Numa and Tarquinius Priscus, the former a Sabine, the latter of mixed Greek and Etruscan ancestry. Another point of special interest is that the kings were not of patrician blood. This is manifestly true of Numa and Tarquinius Priscus, who were immigrants, and of Servius Tullius, about whom one of the few things on which our sources agree is that he was not of patrician birth. . . .

This is unlikely to be an accident, and it prompts the suggestion that the king of Rome had to be an outsider, and that members of the native (patrician) aristocracy were not eligible. . . .

Rome's Kingmakers

The procedures for choosing a king were complex. The key institution was the *interregnum*. When a king died, the patrician heads of families (*patres*) took turns to hold office as *interrex* ('between-king'), each serving for five days. According to Livy the *interregnum* lasted for a year, after which an election was held. The process thus involved both the patricians and the people's assembly. It is not clear from the sources whether the people were merely asked to give assent to a single candidate who had been selected in advance by the *patres*, or whether they were given a genuine choice between candidates. . . . In any event, the *patres* themselves had subsequently to ratify the people's decision. This was the so-called *auctoritas patrum*, which until 339 BC was necessary before any popular decree could become legally binding.

The appointment of a king, therefore, was made 'with the authorisation of the Fathers, by command of the People' (*auctoribus patribus, iussu populi*).

In this process, which was repeated in republican times in the event of the death of both consuls, or if a year ended with no new consuls elected, it is evident that the decisive role was played by the patricians through their control of the *interregnum* and the *auctoritas patrum*. It was the patricians, in short, who chose the king, although it seems clear that they were not themselves eligible for the kingship. This means that the patricians were kingmakers. It also seems that they were . . . the traditional guardians of the auspices (*auspicia*) [methods of reading and interpreting divine signs, or omens]. They conferred the auspices on the king, who held them for life; on his death, 'the auspices returned to the Fathers'. . . . This interesting phrase, which has been the object of much scholarly attention, seems to imply that the patriciate was the ultimate repository of the auspices, and that the king held them in trust. If this interpretation is correct, it would confirm that the king was not himself a patrician or a representative of the *patres*. The king's tenure of the auspices was conferred by a special religious ceremony in which the gods were asked to signify their approval of the new king with favourable omens. . . . In this way the king was 'inaugurated', a word that has passed into our language.

From the sources, then, we can gather that the king was an outsider, sometimes a foreigner, but in any case chosen from outside the patrician aristocracy, and that his election was a complex process involving the previous king, the patricians, the people, and the gods.

Chapter 2

The Early Roman Republic

Turning|Points

IN WORLD HISTORY

Establishment of the Roman Republic

Will Durant

The downfall of the Roman Monarchy circa 509 B.C. brought about the formation of a new government, the Republic, based on the idea of rule by representatives of the people. The Republic would last almost five centuries and oversee Rome's conquest of the Mediterranean world. In this informative tract, the late renowned historian Will Durant ably summarizes Rome's republican system. He begins by citing the first-century B.C. Roman historian Livy's version of the events leading to the Monarchy's fall (which may well be partially legendary), including the famous story of how the son of King Tarquin raised the ire of the nobles by raping the wife of a prominent Roman. Durant then identifies the republican social classes—the aristocratic patricians, common people (plebeians, or plebs), slaves, and so on; discusses the Senate and its considerable powers; and explains the powers and duties of the magistrates (elected public officials).

[In the matter of the birth of the Republic] the tradition becomes literature, and the prose of politics is fused into the poetry of love. One evening (says Livy), in the King's camp at Ardea, his son, Sextus Tarquin, was debating with a relative, Lucius Tarquinius Collatinus, the comparative virtue of their wives. Collatinus proposed that they should take horse to Rome and surprise their ladies in the late hours of the night. They found the wife of Sextus feasting with intimates, but Lucretia, wife of Collatinus, was spinning wool for her husband's clothing. Sextus was inflamed with desire to try

Lucretia's fidelity and enjoy her love. A few days later he returned secretly to the home of Lucretia and overcame her by
wile and force. Lucretia sent for her father and her husband,
told them what had happened, and then stabbed herself to
death. Thereupon Lucius Junius Brutus, a friend of Collatinus, called upon all good men to drive the Tarquins from
Rome. . . . Now he rode with Collatinus to the capital, told
Lucretia's story to the Senate, and persuaded it to banish all
the royal family. The King had meanwhile left the army and
hurried to Rome; Brutus, apprised of this, rode out to the
army, told Lucretia's story again, and won the soldiers' support. Tarquin fled north. . . .

An assembly of the citizen-soldiers was now convened;
and instead of a king chosen for life it elected two consuls,
with equal and rival powers, to rule for a year. These first
consuls, says the tradition, were Brutus and Collatinus; but
Collatinus resigned, and was replaced by Publius Valerius,
who won the name Publicola—"friend of the people"—by
putting through the Assembly several laws that remained
basic in Rome: that any man who should try to make himself
king might be killed without trial; that any attempt to take a
public office without the people's consent should be punish-
able with death; and that any citizen condemned by a magistrate to death or flogging should have the right of appeal
to the Assembly. It was Valerius who inaugurated the custom
whereby a consul, upon entering the Assembly, must part
the axes from the rods and lower them as a sign of the
people's sovereignty and sole right, in peace, to impose a
sentence of death.

The Social Classes

The revolution . . . replaced the monarchy with an aristocracy [of wealthy landowners known as the patricians]. . . .

Who were the patricians? Livy thought that Romulus had
chosen a hundred clan heads of his tribe to help him establish
Rome and be his council or senate. These men were later
called *patres*—"fathers"—and their descendants *patricii*—
"derived from the fathers." . . . We may believe that they were
composed of clans that through economic or military superi-

ority had acquired the best lands, and had transformed their agricultural leadership into political mastery. These victorious clans—the Manlii, Valerii, Aemilii, Cornelii, Fabii, Horatii, Claudii, Julii, etc.—continued for five centuries to give Rome generals, consuls, and laws. . . .

Close to them in wealth, but far below them in political power, were the *equites*, or businessmen. Some were rich enough to win their way into the Senate. . . . These two classes were called the "orders," and were termed *boni*, "the good"; for early civilizations thought of virtue in terms of rank, ability, and power; *virtus* to the Roman meant manliness, the qualities that make a man (*vir*). *Populus*, "people," took in only these upper classes; and originally it was in this sense that those famous initials were used—SPQR (*Senatus Populusque Romanus*)—which were to mark so proudly a hundred thousand monuments. Gradually, as democracy fought its way, the word *populus* came to include the plebs.

This was the main body of Roman citizens. Some were artisans or tradesmen, some were freedmen [ex-slaves], many were peasants; perhaps, in the beginning, they were the conquered natives of the city's hills. Some were attached as

A group of slaves stands on display on a public auction block. Slavery became a major institution in Rome.

clientes, or dependents, to an upper-class *patronus;* in return for land and protection they helped him in peace, served under him in war, and voted in the assemblies as he told them.

Lowest of all were the slaves. Under the kings they had been costly and few, and therefore had been treated with consideration as valuable members of the family. In the sixth century B.C., when Rome began her career of conquest, war captives were sold in rising number to the aristocracy, the business classes, and even to plebeians; and the status of the slave sank. Legally he could be dealt with as any other piece of property; in theory, and according to the custom of the ancients, his life had been forfeited by defeat, and his enslavement was a merciful commutation of his death. Sometimes he managed his master's property, business, or funds; sometimes he became a teacher, writer, actor, craftsman, laborer, tradesman, or artist, and paid his master part of his earnings. In this or other ways he might earn enough to buy his freedom and become a member of the plebs.

The Lower Classes Battle for Their Rights

Contentment is as rare among men as it is natural among animals, and no form of government has ever satisfied its subjects. In this system the businessmen were piqued by their exclusion from the Senate, the richer plebeians by their exclusion from the *equites;* and the poorer plebeians resented their poverty, their political disabilities, and their liability to enslavement for debt. The law of the early Republic allowed a creditor to imprison a persistently defaulting debtor in a private dungeon, to sell him into slavery, even to kill him. Joint creditors might, said the law, cut up the corpse of the defaulting debtor and divide it among them—a provision apparently never enforced. The plebs demanded that these laws should be repealed and the burden of accrued debt reduced; that the lands won in war and owned by the state should be distributed among the poor instead of being given, or sold at nominal prices, to the rich; that plebeians should be eligible to the magistracies and the priesthoods, be permitted to intermarry with the "orders," and have a representative of their class among the highest officials of the government. The Senate sought to frustrate the agitation by fomenting wars, but it was shocked to find its calls to the colors ignored. In 494 B.C. large masses of the plebs "seceded" to the Sacred Mount on the river Anio, three miles from the city, and declared that they would neither fight nor work for Rome until their demands had been met. The Senate used every diplomatic or religious device to lure the rebels back; then, fearing that invasion from without might soon be added to revolt within, it agreed to a cancellation or reduction of debts, and the establishment of two tribunes and three aediles as the elected defenders of the plebs. The plebs returned, but only after taking a solemn oath to kill any man who should ever lay violent hands upon their representatives in the government. . . .

The next step in the climb of the plebs was a demand for definite, written, and secular laws. Heretofore the patrician priests had been the recorders and interpreters of the statutes, had kept their records secret, and had used their monopoly, and the ritual requirements of the law, as weapons against social change. After a long resistance to the new demands, the Senate (454) sent a commission of three patricians to Greece to study and report on the legislation of Solon and other lawmakers. When they returned, the Assembly (451) chose ten men—*decemviri*—to formulate a new code, and gave them supreme governmental power in Rome for two years. This commission, under the presidency of a resolute reactionary, Appius Claudius, transformed the old customary law of Rome into the famous Twelve Tables, submitted them to the Assembly (which passed them with some changes), and displayed them in the Forum for all who would—and could—to read. This seemingly trivial event was epochal in Roman history and in the history of mankind; it was the first written form of that legal structure which was to be Rome's most signal achievement and her greatest contribution to civilization. . . .

It was a major step in the growth of Rome's limited democracy. From that moment the plebs progressed rapidly towards a formal equality with the "orders" in politics and law. In 356 a plebeian was made dictator for a year; in 351 the censorship, in 337 the praetorship, and in 300 the priesthoods were opened to the plebs. Finally (287) the Senate agreed that the decisions of the Tribal Assembly should also have the force of law, even when contrary to the resolutions of the Senate. Since in this Assembly the patricians could easily be outvoted by the plebs, this *lex Hortensia* was the capstone and triumph of Roman democracy.

The Supremacy of the Senate

Nevertheless, the power of the Senate soon recovered after these defeats. The demand for land was quieted by sending Romans as colonists to conquered soil. The cost of winning and holding office—which was unpaid—automatically disqualified the poor. The richer plebeians, having secured political equality and opportunity, now co-operated with the patricians in checking radical legislation; the poorer plebeians, shorn of financial means, ceased for two centuries to play a significant role in the affairs of Rome. Businessmen fell in with patrician policy because it gave them contracts for public works, openings for colonial and provincial exploitation, and commissions to collect taxes for the state. . . . The Senate took the initiative in legislation, and custom sanctioned its authority far beyond the letter of the law. As foreign affairs became more important, the Senate's firm administration of them raised its prestige and power. When, in 264, Rome entered upon a century of war with Carthage for the mastery of the Mediterranean, it was the Senate that led the nation through every trial to victory; and an imperiled and desperate people yielded without protest to its leadership and domination. . . .

The Senate remained supreme. Its original membership of clan heads was recruited by the regular admission of ex-consuls and ex-censors, and the censors were authorized to keep its numbers up to 300 by nominating to it men of patrician or equestrian rank. Membership was for life, but the Senate or a censor could dismiss any member detected in crime or serious moral offense. The august body convened at the call of any major magistrate in the *curia*, or senate house, facing the Forum. By a pleasant custom the members brought their sons with them to attend in silence, and to learn statesmanship and chicanery [dirty dealings] at first hand. Theoretically the Senate might discuss and decide only such issues as were presented to it by a magistrate, and its decisions were merely advice (*senatus consulta*), without the force of law. Actually its prestige was so great that the magistrates nearly always accepted its recommendations, and seldom submitted to the assemblies any measure not already sanctioned by the Senate. Its decisions were subject to veto by any tribune, and a defeated minority of the Senate might appeal to the assemblies; but these procedures were rare except in revolution. The magistrates held power for a year only, while the senators were chosen for life; inevitably this deathless monarch dominated the bearers of a brief authority. The conduct of foreign relations, the making of alliances and treaties, the waging of war, the government of the colonies and provinces, the management and distribution of the public lands, the control of the treasury and its disbursements—all these were exclusive functions of the Senate, and gave it immense power. It was legislature, executive, and judiciary in one. It acted as judge in crimes like treason, conspiracy, or assassination, and appointed from its membership the judges in most major civil trials. When a crisis came it could issue its most formidable decree, the *senatus-consultum ultimum*, "that the consuls should see to it that no harm should come to the state"—a decree that established martial law and gave the consuls absolute command of all persons and property. . . .

The Consuls and Other Public Officials

The major officials were elected by the Centurial, the minor by the Tribal, Assembly. Each office was held by a *collegium* of two or more colleagues, equal in power. All offices except the censorship ran for only a year. The same office could be held by the same person only once in ten years; a year had to elapse between leaving one office and taking another; and in the interval the ex-official could be prosecuted for malfeasance [corruption]. The aspirant to a political career, if he survived a decade in the army, might seek election as one of the quaestors who, under the Senate and the consuls, managed the expenditure of state funds, and assisted the praetors in preventing and investigating crime. If he pleased his electors or his influential supporters, he might later be chosen one of the four aediles charged with the care of buildings, aqueducts, streets, markets, theaters, brothels, saloons, police courts, and public games. If again successful, he might be made one of the four praetors who in war led armies, and in peace acted as judges and interpreters of the law.

At about this point in the *cursus honorum*, or sequence of offices, the citizen who had made a name for integrity and judgment might become one of the two censors ("valuators") chosen every fifth year by the Centurial Assembly. One of them would take the quinquennial census of the citizens, and assess their property for political and military status and for taxation. The censors were required to examine the character and record of every candidate for office; they watched over the honor of women, the education of children, the treatment of slaves, the collection or farming of taxes, the construction of public buildings, the letting of governmental property or contracts, and the proper cultivation of the land. They could lower the rank of any citizen, or remove any member of the Senate, whom they found guilty of immorality or crime; and in this function the power of either censor was immune to the veto of the other. They could try to check extravagance by raising taxes on luxuries. They prepared and published a budget of state expenditures on a five-year plan. At the close of their eighteen-month term they would gather the citizens together in a solemn ceremony of national purification (*lustrum*), as a means of maintaining cordial relations with the gods. Appius Claudius Caecus (the Blind), great-grandson of the Decemvir, was the first to make the censorship rival the consulate in dignity. During his term (312) he built the Appian Aqueduct and the Appian Way, promoted rich plebeians to the Senate, reformed land laws and state finances, [and] helped to break down the priestly and patrician monopoly and manipulation of the law. . . .

Theoretically one of the two consuls ("consultants") had to be a plebeian; actually very few plebeians were chosen, for even the plebs preferred men of education and training for an office that would have to deal with every executive phase of peace and war throughout the Mediterranean. . . . The candidate appeared in person, dressed in a plain white (*candidus*) toga to emphasize the simplicity of his life and morals, and perhaps the more easily to show the scars he had won in the field. If elected, he entered office on the ensuing March 15. The consul took on sanctity by leading the state in the most solemn religious rites. In peace he summoned and presided over the Senate and the Assembly, initiated legislation, administered justice, and in general executed the laws. In war he levied armies, raised funds, and shared with his fellow consul command of the legions. . . .

The consul was limited by the equal authority of his colleague, by the pressure of the Senate, and by the veto power of the tribune. After 367 B.C. fourteen military tribunes were chosen to lead the tribes in war, and ten "tribunes of the plebe" to represent them in peace. These ten were *sacrosancti*: it was a sacrilege, as well as a capital crime, to lay violent hands upon them except under a legitimate dictatorship. Their function was to protect the people against the government, and to stop by one word—*veto*, "I forbid"—the whole machinery of the state, whenever to any one of them this seemed desirable. As a silent observer the tribune could attend the meetings of the Senate, report its deliberations to the people, and, by his veto, deprive the Senate's decisions of all legal force. The door of his inviolable home remained open day and night to any citizen who sought his protection or his aid, and this right of sanctuary or asylum provided the equivalent of *habeas corpus*. Seated on his *tribunal* he could act as judge, and from his decision there was no appeal except to the Assembly of the Tribes. It was his duty to secure the accused a fair trial, and, when possible, to win some pardon for the condemned.

How did the aristocracy retain its ascendancy despite these obstructive powers? First, by limiting them to the city of Rome and to times of peace; in war the tribunes obeyed the consuls. Secondly, by persuading the Tribal Assembly to elect wealthy plebeians as tribunes; the prestige of wealth and the diffidence of poverty moved the people to choose the rich to defend the poor. Thirdly, by allowing the number of tribunes to be raised from four to ten; if only one of these ten would listen to reason or money, his veto could frustrate the rest. In the course of time the tribunes became so dependable that they could be trusted to convene the Senate, take part in its deliberations, and become life members of it after their terms.

If all these maneuvers failed, a last bulwark of social order remained—dictatorship. The Romans recognized that in times of national chaos or peril their liberties and privileges, and all the checks and balances that they had created for their own protection, might impede the rapid and united action needed to save the state. In such cases the Senate could declare an emergency, and then either consul could name a dictator. In every instance but one the dictators came from the upper classes; but it must be said that the aristocracy rarely abused the possibilities of this office. The dictator received almost complete authority over all persons and property, but he could not use public funds without the Senate's consent, and his term was limited to six months or a year. All dictators but two obeyed these restrictions, honoring the story of how Cincinnatus, called from the plow to save the state (456 B.C.), returned to his farm as soon as the task was done. When this precedent was violated by Sulla and Caesar, the Republic passed back into the monarchy out of which it had come.

The Early Roman Army

Peter Connolly

One of the major keys to Rome's successful expansion in Italy during the early republican centuries (as well as later, when it ventured beyond Italy) was the strength and flexibility of its military system, which eventually became world renowned. The armies of the Monarchy and early Republic fought in the Greek-style phalanx. This was a battlefield formation made up of several files (rows) of soldiers, one file behind another, with each soldier wielding a thrusting spear and carrying a round shield. Penetrating this solid mass of men and metal was difficult, and when the phalanx marched forward at an enemy, it could be a considerably formidable force. However, the phalanx was also rather inflexible and did not work well unless the ground was flat and free of obstacles. So the Romans decided to abandon it in favor of a grouping of smaller tactical units that were more mobile and flexible. In the following summary of the early Roman army and the changes it underwent, noted ancient military historian Peter Connolly begins with the original organization of Roman military units into centuries, groups of one hundred (later eighty) men. Then he explains why the Romans abandoned the phalanx and describes the new weapons and tactics that soon made the Roman army the most efficient and successful in the Mediterranean world.

The origins of the Roman military system are lost in prehistory. It is not until Rome comes under Etruscan rule in the 6th century BC that we obtain our first glimpse of the army which was to dominate the Mediterranean for 600 years.

The Greek-style phalanx which the Etruscans had adopted

Excerpted from "The Early Roman Army" by Peter Connolly, in *Warfare in the Ancient World*, edited by John Hackett. Copyright © 1989 by Sidgwick & Jackson Limited. Reprinted by permission of Facts On File, Inc.

during the 7th century, formed the core of the Etrusco-Roman army. It was supported by Latin/Roman contingents who fought on the wings with spears, axes and javelins in their freer native style. The use of native troops to fight alongside their own forces was probably typical of the Etruscan system. This system was later adopted by the Romans.

The ancient historians Livy and Dionysius of Halicarnassus give a relatively detailed description of the Etrusco-Roman army as it was reorganized by [the Roman king] Servius Tullius in the middle of the 6th century. Servius' reorganization, which served both a political and a military purpose, ignored the racial make-up of the society. He divided the population into seven groups according to wealth; the wealth criterion was of crucial military importance, as the individual had to supply his own equipment.

1. *The equites* were the wealthiest citizens grouped into 18 centuries [units of 100 soldiers]. They formed the cavalry, supplying their own horses.

2. *The first class* (the next wealthiest) were formed into 80 centuries of spearmen fully armed with helmet, cuirass, greaves and round shield.

3. *The second class* were divided into 20 centuries of spearmen armed with helmet, greaves and Italian shield *(scutum)*.

4. *The third class* were also divided into 20 centuries of spearmen but were armed only with helmet and Italian shield.

5. *The fourth class*, also 20 centuries, were armed only with spear and Italian shield.

6. *The fifth class*, also 20 centuries, were armed only with slings and javelins.

7. *Capite censi*, literally a 'head count' of all those with little or no property. They had no incentive to defend the state and were considered unfit to serve in the army. This group was to play an increasingly important role in the 3rd to 1st centuries BC as the state tried desperately to keep pace with the army's insatiable demand for manpower.

The 80 centuries of fully armed spearmen with round shields who formed the first class are clearly a Greek-style phalanx. The other four classes, armed in Italian style, are support troops fighting either on the wings or in front of the phalanx before the battle began.

The Latin League

At the end of the 6th century BC the Etruscans were driven out by the combined forces of the Latin towns and the Greeks who had colonized the coastline south of Latium. The victorious Latin towns formed an alliance against the Etruscans known as the Latin League. Rome was a founder member of this alliance. Initially the Etruscans posed the main threat to the League and the phalanx remained the basis of the Latin armies. However, there was a fundamental difference between Greece and Italy; the Etruscans, Latins and Greeks apart, Italy was divided into peoples and tribes rather than city-states. Set-piece battles, in which both sides formed up on mutually acceptable ground, seldom took place in Italy and the effectiveness of the phalanx was therefore limited.

As Etruscan power began to wane, the Latins increasingly turned their attention towards the hill peoples of the east, where the terrain was unsuitable for phalanx warfare. These hill peoples appear to have fought in loose formation, using javelins rather than spears, and the Latins must have been forced to adapt their methods to combat them. It is probable that as early as the middle of the 5th century the phalanx was already giving way to the more flexible system which was to characterize the Roman army.

At the beginning of the 4th century two significant events took place; the army began receiving pay and the phalanx was abandoned. The ancient sources connect both these events with the capture of the Etruscan city of Veii, which fell after a long siege in 396 BC. The first of these reforms could well be the logical result of a long siege which demanded that the soldiers, who would normally serve only in the summer months and so be free to sow and reap their crops, remain in arms all the year round. Pay represented compensation for the loss of their crops. The second is more difficult to understand as battle tactics have no relevance to siege warfare. In truth, it probably relates to an entirely sep-

arate event which occurred in the same area six years later—
the disaster on the Allia.

Throughout the 5th century the Celts (the Romans called
them Gauls) had been seeping through the Alps from Aus-
tria and settling in the Po Valley. They gradually took over
the area, driving out the Etruscans and advancing down the
Adriatic coast. In 390 one of the Celtic tribes, the Senones,
crossed the Appennine Mountains and descended the valley
of the Tiber. The Latin army sent to repel the invaders was
cut to pieces on the banks of the Allia, just 17 km north of
Rome, and the city itself was sacked. It was Rome's most hu-
miliating defeat. The Latins were compelled to conduct an
inquest and take the necessary precautions to prevent a rep-
etition of the disaster. The Etruscans were no longer a serious threat to the Latins. The combined assault from the
Celts in the north and the Latins in the south had broken
their power. The main enemies of the Latins were now the

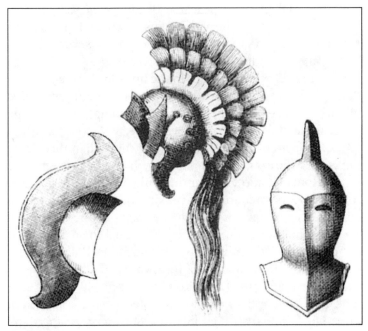

*Early Roman soldiers likely wore helmets like these, developed by the Etrus-
cans, who became Rome's enemy.*

Sabellian hill tribes and the Celts. The Latins were intelligent enough to adapt to the situation, and the Greek-style phalanx was abandoned.

New Weapons and Tactics

The hoplite phalanx was essentially a defensive system designed to combat a frontal attack with spears and javelins. The Celts introduced a new form of fighting into Italy. They were much taller than the Italians and fought primarily with slashing swords. The direction of the Celtic attack was therefore from above or from the side but not from the front. The round hoplite shield proved to be of limited effect against such an attack, whereas the traditional Italian body shield, the *scutum*, with its curved resilient sides and spindle boss, was much more efficient. This shield, reinforced with a metal rim at the top and bottom, now became part of the standard equipment of the heavy infantry.

A new tactic also seems to have evolved. The well-armoured Italian-style spearmen of the *second class* (*hastati*) were re-armed with heavy javelins (*pila*) and placed out ahead of the heavy-armed spearmen of the *first class*. The job of the *hastati* was to break up the force of the Celtic charge and then retreat through gaps in the line of spearmen behind them. This is pure speculation as the sparse and unreliable literary sources of the period tell us nothing, but a change along these lines must have taken place.

The Roman historian Livy, writing more than three centuries after the event he is describing, gives us a brief glimpse of the Roman/Latin army in the middle of the 4th century, some 50 years after the changes outlined above must have taken place. Historians have made much of the contradictions in Livy's account, and have even tried to adapt it to fit the description given by the Greek historian Polybius, who described the Roman army of his own day (*c.* 130 BC).

Livy, describing the Latin-Roman army in 340 when Rome took command of the Latin League, states that it consisted of three lines of heavy-armed infantry, the *triarii*, *principes* and *hastati*, supported by troops who appear to be progressively lighter armed, the *rorarii*, *accensi* and *leves*, the last being skirmishers. The *triarii* and *principes* appear to be the old Servian *first class*. The *hastati*, as their name suggests, were probably the old Italian-style spearmen of the *second class*. The *rorarii*, *accensi* and *leves* were the old *third, fourth* and *fifth class* respectively. These last three groups probably still fought on the wings and in front as they had in the old days.

The *triarii*, although armed with the Italian shield (*scutum*), still fight as a phalanx but are much reduced in numbers and have a purely defensive role. The *principes*, like the *hastati*, are now armed with heavy javelins and fight out ahead of the spearmen as a second advanced line.

The use of the *hastati* re-armed with javelins had clearly worked and the Romans must have decided to add a similarly armed second line (*principes*). After throwing their javelins the *hastati* drew their swords and charged in to close quarters, taking advantage of the confusion caused by the hail of javelins. If this failed to break the enemy, they retreated through the gaps between the *principes*, who then mounted a similar charge. Usually these two assaults were sufficient to defeat the enemy. However, if both lines were overcome, they would retreat through gaps in the *triarii*, who would then close ranks, level their spears and retreat to the safety of the camp. The *triarii* were the last line of defence, saving the army when the battle was lost. The Roman saying 'it has come to the *triarii*' implied a desperate situation.

In an era of varying fortune when the prospect of defeat must have been a constant nightmare, it is not surprising that the new army retained a strong defensive third line. At some point over the next 70 years the *rorarii* and *accensi* were absorbed into the *hastati* and *leves* respectively and half the *triarii* joined the *principes*, producing the army that was known to Polybius. This change may have come soon after Rome took over the Latin League, for the Latin allies of Rome formed the wings of the Roman army, making the *rorarii* and *accensi* redundant. The change must have taken place well before 256 because in this year Polybius describes the Roman fleet taking up the traditional Roman legionary formation of *triarii*, *principes* and *hastati*.

Rome Unifies the Italian Peninsula

Chester G. Starr

During the first two centuries or so of its existence the Roman Republic expanded its power and influence steadily outward until it had acquired control of all Italy. The major events of this extraordinary achievement are summarized here by former University of Michigan scholar Chester G. Starr. As he explains, the members of the Latin League (a loose confederation of early Latin towns, of which Rome was a member), the Etruscans, Samnites, Greeks, and others fell, one by one, under Roman domination. Starr also provides an excellent analysis of the reasons for Rome's success, including its superior army organization and its lenient policies toward the peoples it conquered.

While the Romans culturally fell into a backwater, their political and military abilities were never more marked than from the era from 509 to 264 B.C. During this dimly lit period they . . . went on to conquer all the peninsula. Internally they hammered out, slowly and with many false starts, a reorganization of their political system which eventually produced technical democracy.

Down to 340 B.C. the wars of the Early Republic took place in a narrow strip of western Italy, 30 miles from the sea to the central mountains and go miles from the Ciminian hills of south Etruria to the jutting promontory of Tarracina at the edge of the Latin districts. The main opponents were initially the expanding hill tribes of the Acqui and Volsci, who pressed on both the Latins and the Romans. After the Latin league had secured its independence from Rome at the battle of Lake Regillus (c. 496 B.C.) the two powers none-theless found themselves forced to join in a treaty of equal alliance to oppose the hillsmen. . . . The critical battle appears to have been that of Mt. Algidus in 431, after which the tide turned in favor of the plainsmen.

The Romans were also at odds on their own with the neighboring Etruscan center of Veii, which traded southward across the Tiber via Praeneste. The direct route was cut by Roman advance up the Tiber in 426–25, but reduction of Veii itself was a bitter struggle. In the end Veii was taken in 396 and was utterly destroyed by the general M. Furius Camillus after a continuous siege over several years. During the last stage the Roman state had to institute regular payment for the soldiers thus kept away from their farms.

Then came the worst blow Rome was ever to suffer until its final collapse in the fifth century after Christ. Uncivilized Celts, called Gauls, had been moving down into the Po valley from central Europe and launched a series of great raids into central Italy. In 390, according to conventional Roman chronology, the Roman army marched out to meet the Gauls north of Rome at the Allia river, but was wiped out. The city itself was almost totally destroyed.

The dogged Romans, however, rose nobly to the threat. They appointed Camillus dictator and raised a new army. In 378–57 they built a stone wall five and one-half miles long about the city, far larger than that of any Etruscan city. As defenders of central Italy Rome gained extensive support and by 350 was virtually master of the neighborhood.

Masters of the Peninsula

To lay a solid basis for further expansion had required almost two centuries, but now the Romans blazed forth. During the period 340 to 264 they conquered all the rest of the Italian peninsula. The initial stimulus came from a revolt of the Latin league, which chafed at its increasingly dependent position; in a brief war, 340–38, the Romans defeated and dissolved the league. During the hostilities with the Latins, their southern neighbors, the wealthy Oscans who had become civilized in Campania [the fertile region south of

Latium] appealed again for assistance against their Samnite kinsmen of the central mountains. Capua, Cumae, and other cities were accordingly added to Roman control.

This latter step brought the Romans by 326 into serious conflict with the Samnites, who were far more numerous but less well unified. Although the first phase ended in 321 when the Samnites trapped a Roman army at the Caudine forks, the wars flared up again and again. It was probably in this long-protracted struggle that the Romans reorganized their basic military unit, the legion, into a more supple structure. During the Samnite wars they had also to face from time to time Etruscan and Gallic foes; but they skillfully divided and conquered their enemies, while their own subjects generally remained loyal. The Roman victory at Sentinum in 295 delivered the crucial blow to an army of Samnites and Gauls; final settlement, however, scarcely came until 282.

There remained southern Italy, where the Greek cities of the coast were barely maintaining themselves against inland Lucanian tribes. In 282 Rome sent an army south at the request of Thurii and dispatched a few ships to the gulf off Tarentum, in violation of an old agreement with that state. The Tarentines sank the ships and invited into Italy the king of [the Greek Kingdom of] Epirus, Pyrrhus (319–272). This skilled Hellenistic general defeated the Romans at Heraclea (280) and Asculum (279), partly through using the new tactical weapon of elephants.

Pyrrhus then essayed to make peace. The Senate almost approved his terms; but the Carthaginians hastily offered Rome naval and financial aid, and an aged Roman leader, Appius Claudius, had himself carried into the Senate House to speak against compromise. Since Pyrrhus could not hope to conquer all central Italy from the Romans, he turned to Sicily upon the invitation of the Greeks in the islands and fought the Carthaginians. When he returned to Italy in 275, the Romans checked him at Beneventum; Pyrrhus withdrew to Epirus; and the Greek cities of the south had to admit Roman garrisons. Thenceforth the Romans were masters of the Italian peninsula.

The Roman conquest of Italy was not a process the Romans deliberately planned, for it took over two centuries of almost haphazard actions. If the Romans fought so continuously, the reasons lie partly in the ill-stabilized conditions. In Italy at this time strife between plainsmen and hillsmen was unending and opened the way for the Gauls; the Greeks quarreled among themselves and tempted intervention by their Italic neighbors. The Roman system of alliances, which made Rome responsible for protecting each ally, also involved Rome in an ever-widening circle of external entanglements.

Potent forces of expansion existed within Rome itself. The Romans remembered their days of greatness in the kingdom; their leaders sought military glory, which would enhance the honor of their families and bring them booty; and the population of Rome seems to have increased at a rapid rate. Beside looting their victims of movable property, the Romans commonly took about a third of conquered lands on which they settled colonies of Roman and Latin farmers.

To explain their victories, the Romans had one fundamental answer: "We have overcome all the nations of the world, because we have realized that the world is directed and governed by the gods [Cicero, *On the Responses of the Haruspices* 9]." Divine support was gained by scrupulous attention to religious vows by the leaders and by rewards of booty to the temples; the Romans, too, had a ceremony conducted by the *fetiales* [state priests] which ensured that their wars were just defenses of the Romans and their allies. This religious machinery undoubtedly had a considerable effect in heartening the troops and generals to their tasks, but more earthly factors also had a potent role both in bringing victory and in aiding the maintenance of Roman rule.

A Flexible Military System

Tactically and strategically the Romans hammered out ever more supple principles of organization and operations. Most of their enemies, who were not civilized, could be divided and met in detail by Roman forces, which were kept concentrated and had a central geographical position. Even skilled opponents like Pyrrhus could win only battles, not wars, against the abundance of Roman manpower and the dogged persistence of Roman leadership. Initially the Romans organized their legions into phalanxes, but during the Samnite wars they developed a more articulated division of the legion into blocs or *maniples*, grouped in three lines which operated independently; most soldiers were now armed with short swords and javelins.

As far as possible, the Romans fought only on ground of their own choosing and at the time when they were ready. To aid them in refusing battle under unfavorable circumstances they picked up from Pyrrhus the habit of fortifying their camp every night. Roman commanders were mostly experienced veterans' and since they were also the chief officials of the state they normally could decide on their own judgment when and how to give battle.

Holding down the conquered called for skills of a more political nature. The establishment of colonies provided bases and points of control over conquered areas, and by the late fourth century the Romans had begun to build all-weather roads to link the capital with other districts. Appius Claudius laid out the first great Roman road, the *via Appia*, to Capua in 312. More important, however, was the treatment of the defeated. A Roman conquest was not in itself a gentle matter, and a considerable part of conquered lands was taken for Roman settlers. Yet the Romans generally were fighting peoples of similar culture and language, and after the destruction of Veii they commonly spared the vanquished from utter destruction.

Incorporating Conquered People

Across the fourth century the Romans developed a very deftly arranged set of varying positions for their subjects. Most defeated states became "allies" (*socii*), who paid no tribute and retained local self-government; they furnished a set number of troops upon call and surrendered foreign policy to Rome. After the Latin league was dissolved in 338, many Latin states received "Latin status," holders of which could gain citizenship if they settled in Rome; most colonies also received this status. Dating from the annexation of Tusculum in 381, however, some Latin communities were absorbed down the years into the Roman citizen territory but retained their legal existence as local *"municipia."* Yet a fourth status, that of Roman citizenship without the right to vote, was given to areas in Campania and elsewhere. By 225 B.C., as we know from a list of [the second-century B.C. Greek historian] Polybius, about 1,000,000 male inhabitants of Italy were Roman citizens (either full citizens, full citizens having a local center in their *municipium*, or citizens without a vote), 500,000 were Latins, and 1,500,000 were allies, grouped in some 120 to 150 small states.

Thereby the Romans bound particularly the upper classes in the subject territories to their rule and divided Italy so that it could not feel a sense of common opposition to a tyrannical master. Unwittingly the Romans began thus to enlarge the concept of Rome and so took great steps toward solving the problem of welding conquered to home territories, a problem which had shattered the Athenian empire. One of Rome's opponents [Macedonia's King Philip V] was later to praise this liberality in granting citizenship. . . . Eventually in A.D. 212 Roman citizenship was to be given to virtually all free men of the entire Mediterranean basin.

Rome's First Military Encounter with the Greeks

John Warry

By the start of the third century B.C., the two leading military systems in the Mediterranean world were the Greek phalanx (recently modified as the "Macedonian phalanx," which featured soldiers in the formation's rear rows carrying longer and longer spears), and the Roman legions. Throughout most of the known world, the Greek system was considered to be the superior one. Outside of Italy, Rome was still viewed by many as an overrated upstart. This assessment was based in large degree on the fact that the two systems had never clashed in a major battle. The Romans first met the renowned Greek phalanx when they took on Pyrrhus, king of the small Greek kingdom of Epirus (in northwestern Greece), whom a Greek city in southern Italy had begged to defend it against the encroaching Romans. The upshot is that Pyrrhus managed to gain some victories over the Romans; but they were very costly and foreshadowed the difficulties the Greeks would encounter later against Rome. The following concise account of Pyrrhus's Italian adventures is by former Cambridge University scholar John Warry. The ancient sources that Warry draws on include the life of Pyrrhus by the first-century A.D. Greek biographer Plutarch, and information from two earlier Greek chroniclers, Dionysius (first century B.C.) and Hieronymous (third century B.C.).

In the middle of the fourth century BC, the Dorian Greek colonists of Tarentum in southern Italy had appealed to Sparta, their mother city, for help against the indigenous population which threatened them. At a time when northern Greece was crucially involved against Philip of Macedon, Sparta had sent a force under King Archidamus III, who had subsequently been killed fighting in Italy. Later, when Alexander the Great was in the east, his mother's brother, also named Alexander, who had made himself ruler of the tribes and cities of Epirus, gladly accepted another Tarentine invitation to intervene in southern Italy. He too was killed fighting there. A third episode of this kind occurred in 303 BC, when Cleonymus, a Spartan mercenary general, with 5,000 men, championed the Tarentines against Italian neighbours. Cleonymus used Italy as a base against Corcyra (Corfu) and eventually quarreled with the city which had engaged him. For Tarentum, the most natural sources of Greek aid in these recurrent situations were Sparta, their mother city, and Epirus, conveniently situated opposite the heel of Italy across comparatively narrow seas. In 281 BC, at last in open conflict with Rome, the Tarentines issued an invitation to King Pyrrhus of Epirus. . . .

Pyrrhus Crosses to Italy

Pyrrhus inherited his title to the throne as a child and as a consequence his position long remained precarious. However, he at last enlisted the help of Ptolemy and, after establishing himself powerfully in Epirus, ruled at first jointly and then as sole monarch. In this capacity, he allied himself with the Thracian dynast Lysimachus to drive out Demetrius, who had claimed the throne of Macedon on the death of Cassander in 287 BC. Demetrius' claim was based on his marriage to Antipater's daughter Phila and he derived support from some of the Greek states, to whom he had at one time presented himself as a champion of constitutional liberty. Pyrrhus and Lysimachus, in combination, succeeded in defeating Demetrius, but when the victors competed for domination of the Macedonian kingdom, Pyrrhus was forced to withdraw. Thus frustrated, he was ready to direct his ambitions westwards.

The Tarentines, who gave Pyrrhus his opportunity, had an old treaty with Rome, perhaps describable as obsolete, according to which the Romans were not to send warships into the Tarentine Gulf. In 282 BC the Romans installed supporting garrisons in the Greek cities of Thurii, Locri and Rhegium. These measures were directed against the Italian people of Lucania, to the north. Thurii, however, lay at the western corner of the Tarentine Gulf and, probably as a demonstration of strength, the Romans sent warships there.

The matter could have been overlooked by the Tarentines, but they were already anxious at the expansion of Roman power and decided on war. They accordingly attacked and sank several Roman warships, drove the Roman garrison from Thurii and sacked the city. The violence of their reaction may be explained ideologically by the hatred of Tarentine democrats for Thurian oligarchs. Committed now to war against Rome, the Tarentines made their invitation to Pyrrhus not only in their own name but on behalf of other Greek cities in Italy. As a contribution to the common war effort, they offered both their own armed forces and substantial levies of indigenous Italian troops. . . .

Pyrrhus immediately sent Cineas, his Thessalian staff officer and diplomat on whose education and intelligence he placed great reliance, to Tarentum with an advance party of 3,000 men, while he himself assembled the main body of the invasion forces. Vessels for the convoy and an accompanying escort of war galleys were provided by Tarentum itself. In the past, Cleonymus had been similarly supplied. In a fleet which included horse-transports and a variety of flat-bottomed boats, Pyrrhus embarked 20 elephants, 3,000 cavalry, 20,000 infantry, 2,000 archers and 500 slingers. . . .

The Battle of Heraclea

As the king approached Tarentum, Cineas came out to meet him with such forces as were already stationed in the city. Whatever the precise terms of Pyrrhus' agreement with the Tarentines, he was very careful not to do anything which might offend them until his own widely dispersed fleet had at last made its way into harbour at Tarentum. He then took charge of the situation, placed the whole city on a war footing, closed all places of entertainment and sport, suspended all festivities and social events and conscripted the population for military service. Some of the citizens, who objected very strongly to this treatment, left the town.

Pyrrhus soon learned that a formidable Roman army was approaching, plundering the Lucanian hinterland on its way. The large force of allies which had been promised him by the Tarentines had not yet arrived, and Pyrrhus would gladly have waited until he had the support of greater numbers. To delay longer, however, leaving all initiative to the enemy, would clearly have been strategically inadvisable and bad for morale. He therefore led out his men to confront the Romans. Perhaps for the sake of further procrastination, he sent forward a herald to enquire whether the enemy would accept him as an arbitrator of their differences with Tarentum. The reply was, as at this stage he might have expected, that the Romans neither wanted him as an arbitrator nor feared him as an enemy.

Pyrrhus watched from his camp near Heraclea as the Romans crossed the river Siris and was impressed by their good order and military discipline, which, as he remarked to one of his officers, seemed surprising in "barbarians". More than ever, he was disposed to wait for his reinforcements, but this was precisely what the Romans were determined to prevent him from doing. Pyrrhus deployed his men along the river bank in defensive positions, but the Romans were beforehand. Their infantry crossed the river at fordable points in some strength, and Pyrrhus' men, threatened with encirclement, had to withdraw.

In the circumstances which we have just outlined, the battle of Heraclea began. Pyrrhus realized that he must seize the initiative without further delay and, adopting the time-honoured tactics of the great Alexander, left his phalanx to hold the enemy in front, while he himself led a cavalry charge at the head of 3,000 horses. But unlike Alexander, he had timed the move badly. His attack came too late. The Romans themselves were usually weak in cavalry, but on this occasion they seem to have been well supported by the horsemen of their Italian allies, and Pyrrhus' Thessalian cavalry were driven back. The king then ordered his phalangists [phalanx men] to attack, though an offensive role was not normal or suitable for them and they might well have found themselves encircled by the opposing cavalry if the enemy's horses had

A Costly Victory

This is Plutarch's account of the second day of fighting at Ausculum, including Pyrrhus's famous remark that later inspired the term "Pyrrhic victory," meaning something won at great cost.

The next day Pyrrhus regrouped his forces so as to fight on even terrain, where his elephants could be used against the enemy's line. At first light he detached troops to occupy the difficult ground, posted strong contingents of archers and slingers in the spaces between the elephants, and then launched his main body into the attack in close order and with an irresistible impetus. The Romans could not employ the feinting and skirmishing tactics they had used on the previous day and were compelled to receive Pyrrhus' charge on level ground and head on. They were anxious to repulse Pyrrhus' heavy infantry before the elephants came up, and so they hacked desperately with their swords against the Greek pikes, exposing themselves recklessly, thinking only of killing and wounding the enemy and caring nothing for their own losses. After a long struggle, so it is said, the Roman line began to give way at the point where Pyrrhus himself was pressing his opponents hardest, but the factor which did most to enable the Greeks to prevail was the weight and fury of the elephants' charge. Against this even the Romans' courage was of little avail: they felt as if they might have done before the rush of a tidal wave or the shock of an earthquake, that it was better to give way than to stand their ground to no purpose, and suffer a terrible fate without gaining the least advantage. . . .

The two armies disengaged and the story goes that when one of Pyrrhus' friends congratulated him on his victory, he replied, 'One more victory like that over the Romans will destroy us completely!'

Plutarch, *Life of Pyrrhus*, in *The Age of Alexander: Nine Greek Lives by Plutarch*. Trans. Ian Scott-Kilvert. New York: Penguin, 1973, pp. 408–409.

not taken fright at the elephants and become uncontrollable. In these circumstances, the Thessalian cavalry was able to resume the offensive and soon carried all before it.

The victory, though not decisive, was something better than what we usually describe as "Pyrrhic". Roman casualties were, according to Dionysius, 15,000; according to Hieronymus, 7,000. Pyrrhus' casualties were, by Dionysius' account, 13,000; by Hieronymus', 4,000. Perhaps we should not sneer at such widely divergent statistics. Casualty reports from modern theatres of war often show similar discrepancies. In any case, Pyrrhus possessed himself of the abandoned Roman camp, and his prestige was very much enhanced, so that many of the hesitant Lucanians, Samnites and other allies, whom he had awaited in vain before the battle, now joined him.

Another Costly Lesson

Pyrrhus did not expect to take Rome itself, but he advanced northwards, to within 37 miles (60 km) of the city walls, hoping to negotiate out of strength. However, his presence by no means intimidated the Romans. No fear that he would detach their allies from them, ravage their lands or lay siege to the city itself induced them to make peace on terms that would safeguard the Tarentines. Their friendship remained conditional on the unconditional departure of Pyrrhus and his army from Italy.

Meanwhile, two Roman consular armies had been brought up to strength and remained at large in Italy. Pyrrhus could not afford to ignore them. They might threaten his rear; they might threaten his communications; they might threaten his allies. Above all, prestige and morale were at stake. He must not appear reluctant to engage the enemy. He broke off negotiations with the Roman government and went campaigning again. Confronting the Romans at Asculum in Apulia, he fought them on rough and wooded ground which gave little opportunity to his elephants or cavalry and turned the fight into an infantry engagement. The ground seems also to have hampered the phalanx: the Romans prolonged the battle all day, and night fell without a decision having been reached.

On the following day, Pyrrhus contrived to fight on open

ground which was less to the enemy's advantage, giving them no occasion for the tactics of flexible response, such as they had adopted in the wilder country. Even so, the Romans, with their short swords, striving desperately to reach a decision before the elephants could be brought into action, seem to have been a match for the long pikes of the Greek phalanx. In the end, the elephants once more gave Pyrrhus his victory—which this time was more "Pyrrhic" in character. The Romans merely retreated into their camp. Pyrrhus himself was wounded in the arm. Hieronymus' figures are of 6,000 Roman casualties, as compared with 3,550 on Pyrrhus' side. But many of Pyrrhus' ablest officers were among the dead and he was not in a position to recruit new troops, as the Romans were.

Pyrrhus was a brave and inspiring if rather flamboyant commander, who was well capable of keeping his head even in the middle of a most desperate fight. Yet he does not seem to have excelled either as a strategist or a tactician. At Heraclea, by waiting for reinforcements, he conceded a valuable initiative to the Romans, without receiving the reinforcements for which he had waited. The timing of the cavalry charge with which he had opened the battle was also tardy. At Asculum, he could not make the right choice of ground until a day of indecisive fighting had taught him costly lessons. [In another strategically questionable move, Pyrrhus suddenly moved his army to Sicily, where the local Greek cities were menaced by Carthage.] . . .

Pyrrhus Abandons the Italian Greeks

At the time of Pyrrhus' operations in Italy and Sicily (281–275 BC), Rome and Carthage were in fact associated by a series of treaties which dated from very early times. The precise number of these treaties is a subject on which neither ancient historians nor modern scholars agree. . . .

However, the first two . . . treaties seem to have been mainly commercial in scope; the third, military and naval. The underlying principle seems to have been that Carthage should offer naval aid in return for Roman military support.

It is indeed on record that, hoping to hinder Pyrrhus' intervention in Sicily, a Carthaginian admiral arrived with ships to dissuade Rome from making peace with the king. The Romans were not at first willing to commit themselves. The Carthaginians then sailed off to negotiate with Pyrrhus. These negotiations also led to nothing, but when the Carthaginian mission returned again to Rome, the Romans were more amenable. The Carthaginian negotiators had made their point. The 120 ships could be thrown into either scale: Rome continued its war against Pyrrhus' allies in Italy. In fact, the Carthaginian commander, on his way back to Sicily, even transported 500 Roman soldiers to Rhegium, on the straits of Messina, in order to reinforce the garrison.

The Carthaginian diplomatic initiative against Pyrrhus certainly seems to have borne fruit. Moreover, the Carthaginian navy attacked the king's forces as they returned from Sicily and destroyed a substantial number of his ships. . . .

In Italy, the Samnites, disgusted by Pyrrhus' neglect of their cause, were no longer willing to rally round him in great strength. Two Roman armies, respectively under the two consuls of the year, were now campaigning separately. Pyrrhus detached half his force to deal with the enemy in Lucania, while he himself marched northward to confront the Romans near Malventum (later renamed, more propitiously, Beneventum). Here, he attempted a night attack. Night attacks, in ancient warfare, were notoriously prone to miscarry. . . . Pyrrhus' attempt was no exception to the general rule. His advancing forces lost their way in wooded country during the hours of darkness and at dawn found themselves deployed in positions for which they had never bargained. The Romans, at first alarmed by the unexpected presence of the enemy, soon realized that it was possible to attack the isolated vanguard and rout it. Thus encouraged, the cautious consul gave battle to Pyrrhus' main body in the open plain. On this occasion, the Romans seem to have discovered a method of dealing with elephants: though the animals at first moved onward with their usual irresistible momentum, they were eventually frightened and induced to turn against their own troops. As a consequence, Pyrrhus was obliged to retreat.

He was now left in command of 8,000 infantry and 500 cavalry and, as Plutarch convincingly assures us, for lack of money to pay them, he was obliged to look for a new war. This he found in Macedonia, which Antigonus Gonatas, Demetrius' son and successor, proceeding from his rather precarious foothold in Greece, now occupied. . . . Pyrrhus was successful against Antigonus' elephants and won over the opposing Macedonian infantry by an appeal made to them on the battlefield. Antigonus fled, but the Macedonian population was soon alienated from Pyrrhus. . . .

As ever, turning from a task which, left uncompleted, would have been better unattempted, Pyrrhus answered an invitation to meddle in Spartan politics, hoping thereby to make himself master of the Peloponnese. He was killed in Argos during a street fight, having been felled by an accurately aimed tile from a woman's hand.

Meanwhile, in Italy, the garrison which Pyrrhus had left at Tarentum defied the Romans until 272 BC. It then surrendered, but was allowed to withdraw on honourable terms, while the Tarentines gave hostages to Rome and accepted a Roman garrison. The Romans dealt sternly but not vindictively with the Italian populations which had supported Pyrrhus. Important sectors of their territory were confiscated in order to provide for Latin colonial settlements. . . .

Rome now dominated southern and central Italy, including . . . the Greek cities.

Chapter 3

The Punic Wars

The First Punic War and Its Aftermath

Michael Rostovtzeff

No sooner had the Romans become masters of Italy than they continued their rise to world power by embroiling themselves in a large-scale war with the most powerful empire in the western Mediterranean sphere—Carthage. Before the outbreak of this so-called First Punic War in 264 B.C., Rome already had an alliance with the Greek city of Massilia (on the southern coast of Gaul, what is now France), and also a long-standing treaty with Carthage providing that each would stay out of the other's sphere of influence. But this treaty fell by the wayside when Rome and Carthage came face to face over who should control Sicily (initially fighting over the city of Messana, on the narrow strait of the same name that separates northeastern Sicily from southwestern Italy). The late, great classical historian Michael Rostovtzeff here delivers a clearly-written summary of the events leading to the war; the major goals, victories, and mistakes of the combatants; the amazing Roman determination to succeed even when the chances of doing so seemed slim; the conditions of the peace agreement at war's end; and the subsequent build-up of Carthaginian forces in Spain, which foreshadowed the second great conflict between the two peoples.

After the long and arduous wars which led to the creation of the Italian confederacy, Rome became one of the strongest powers in the civilized world. Her military strength was more considerable than that of any one of the empires which then maintained a balance of power in the East—more con-

From *Rome* by Michael Ivanovich Rostovtzeff, edited by Elias Bickerman, translated by J.D. Duff. Copyright © 1960 by Oxford University Press, Inc. Used by permission of Oxford University Press, Inc.

siderable not so much in point of numbers as in the solidarity, organization, and intelligence of her soldiers. To the troops of the other empires, serving for pay and enlisted by force from the native populations, she could oppose an army as well trained and as numerous, and manned by citizens and allies, who fought, not for money nor by compulsion, but by the voluntary decision of the whole body of Roman citizens.

When Rome defeated Pyrrhus, one of the most gifted Hellenistic [Greek] kings, and thus claimed a place in the family of empires in the third century B.C., this apparition was noted and studied by the Hellenistic statesmen of the time. Macedonia, Italy's nearest neighbour, began to attend to the course of events in Italy; Egypt was the first to enter into diplomatic relations with Rome, in 273 B.C.; and in Greece the Leagues and free communities began to take account of this new power as a possible ally both in their mutual strifes and in the contest carried on by the western Greeks against the growing insolence of the Illyrian pirates. But more than any of these, Carthage, with her commercial and political interests in the western Mediterranean, was affected by the foreign policy of Rome. To her Rome and the political successes of Rome were no novelty. At first she looked on Rome as the successor of Etruria [homeland of the Etruscans] in Italy and hoped that her own trade would not be damaged. For Rome was not a great maritime empire in the fifth and fourth centuries B.C., and owned no fleet either for war or commerce. The trade of the Latin and surviving Etruscan ports kept up its semi-piratical character and could not compete with the trade of Carthage. For this reason Carthage renewed in 348 B.C. the commercial treaty concluded with Rome at the end of the sixth century; and for this reason the commercial treaty was converted in 279 during the war with Pyrrhus into a military alliance against the common enemy. It is clear that Carthage still regarded Rome as a counterpoise to the Greek cities, just as she had regarded Etruria at an earlier date.

The Two Sides Evenly Matched

But the position was altered when all the harbours of south Italy were annexed to the empire of Rome, and when the interests of Naples and Tarentum, those ancient rivals of Carthage, became the interests of Rome also. It became clear to Carthage that Rome, as the leader of the western Greeks [i.e., the Greek cities of Italy], was bound in the near future to take a hand in Sicilian affairs and to support the Sicilian Greeks in their secular struggle with the Carthaginians. It was significant that Rome had long been the ally of Massilia, the other Greek rival that Carthage feared. It must also be observed that relations between the Sicilian Greeks and the native Italian tribes, always frequent and uninterrupted, were especially active in the fourth century B.C. Detachments of Samnites were frequently hired for military service in Sicily, and many of them, after a period of service, were rewarded by their employers with allotments of land. A striking instance of the Samnite desire to establish themselves in Sicily is afforded by the history of the Greek city of Messana. It was seized by Samnite mercenaries in the pay of Agathocles and converted into a Samnite city—a fate which had long before befallen Rhegium, a Greek city on the eastern side of the Straits.

Thus the collision between Rome and Carthage was inevitable; and the sooner it came, the better for Carthage. The strength of the rivals was nearly equal. Both powers were based on a community of citizens and originally relied on a citizen army, numerous and well trained. Both powers had allies, who were bound to contribute their forces in case their principal was involved in war against any enemy whatever. On one side were Etruscans, Samnites, Umbrians, and Italian Greeks, while the African Empire of Carthage could count on the Berbers or Libyans who inhabited her territory, and on the Numidians who were neighbours and tributaries; and both these were warlike nations and by no means uncivilized. In neither case was there any strong feeling of attachment on the part of the allies to their principal; still, under ordinary circumstances, both Rome and Carthage could reckon on their support. Carthage had better cavalry than Rome and more of it, and her infantry was armed as efficiently. She had also a large body of excellently trained mercenaries, who had passed through the severe school of Hellenistic warfare, and a considerable number of armed elephants—a recent addition to the fighting power of Hellenistic armies. Indeed, in every branch of tactics studied by the Hellenistic generals, and especially in engineering, the Carthaginians were even superior to the Romans. Lastly, they had a powerful fleet and great wealth. Nevertheless, when it came to fighting on land, the Romans had considerable advantages. For at this time the citizens of Carthage hardly ever served in the ranks, and their places were filled by mercenaries and allies who were liable to fail at the critical moment; whereas the Roman army contained no mercenaries and consisted entirely of citizens and allies; and some of the latter, for instance, the Latins, were no less to be trusted than Roman citizens themselves.

This equality of strength made it impossible to foresee which antagonist would prove victorious. The contest was bound to begin in Sicily, and the attitude of the Sicilian Greeks was of great importance. It so happened that just at this time they had found once again an able and prudent leader in Hiero II, tyrant of Syracuse, who had seized control of the city in 269 B.C. He had then, following the example of Agathocles and Pyrrhus, declared himself king of Sicily and had subdued several of the neighbouring cities.

The Outbreak of War

The war began in 264 B.C. and, as always happens in similar cases, on a comparatively trifling pretext. The Samnites, who had taken Messana in 289 B.C. and now called themselves Mamertini, lived by plundering the Greek cities in their neighbourhood. When Hiero, wishing to stop their depredations, laid siege to Messana, a section of the inhabitants appealed to Carthage for help. This opportunity of occupying the city was welcomed, and a Carthaginian garrison was sent: it was important for Carthage to establish herself on the Straits of Messina in close proximity to her ancient enemy, Syracuse. But a majority of the Mamertines sought aid from Rome. The Romans understood that to help the Mamertines meant war with Carthage. But on the other hand, if Carthage controlled the Straits, the vital interests of

Rome were affected: not only would her shipping be subject to interference in the straits, but also it would be possible, in case of need, to land a foreign army in Italy. After some hesitation Rome determined on war and sent a strong army into Sicily. The Mamertines then obliged the Carthaginian garrison to decamp and surrendered their city to the Romans.

Confronted by a common danger, Hiero and the Carthaginians made an alliance; but their armies failed to take Messana. After this failure, Hiero abandoned his ally and took sides with the Romans: they seemed to him more powerful, and they promised, if victorious, not only to recognize his rule over Syracuse and his independence, but also to extend his kingdom at the cost of the Carthaginian dominions in Sicily. When this treaty was once made, the king remained faithful to it throughout the war; and the Romans were greatly indebted to him for their final victory. Without his aid Rome could hardly have solved the problem of feeding her army, and Syracuse was essential as a station for the Roman fleet. We shall see later how the struggle with Carthage forced the Romans to create a powerful navy.

The war for Sicily dragged on for twenty-three years, from 264 to 241 B.C., with hardly a break. The antagonists put forth every effort, and both sides revealed a remarkable genius for war and sent out great generals to command their armies. Neither the Graeco-Oriental monarchies nor Macedonia and Greece took any part in the conflict. The feeling of the Hellenistic world was neutral, and not one of the Hellenistic monarchies was directly interested in the result. Ptolemy Philadelphus, king of Egypt, was the nearest neighbour of Carthage; and it is an interesting fact that he kept up friendly relations with both the combatants.

Why Rome Won the War

The victory of Rome in the first Punic war—this name was used by the Romans who called the Carthaginians *Poeni* or Phoenicians—was due chiefly to a number of mistakes made by the Carthaginians at the very beginning. In spite of their original superiority at sea, they suffered the Roman armies to cross from Italy into Sicily; they were unable to retain Hiero's support; and they failed to send a force sufficient to destroy the first Roman detachments that landed in the island. The Romans, on their side, surprised Carthage by their activity at sea. Helped by Sicilian and Italian Greeks they built a large fleet, and equipped their ships with a contrivance unknown to the Carthaginians, which they probably owed to Greek engineers—bridges [called "ravens"] for boarding the enemy ships, which enabled the heavy-armed Roman infantry to fight just as they were accustomed to fight on dry land.

Thanks to these mistakes on the part of Carthage and the strength of their own fleet, the Romans were able to drive the enemy out of many Sicilian cities and to win a series of decisive victories by sea. Encouraged by these successes, Rome hoped to end the war with one blow, and sent a fairly strong army to Africa in 256 B.C. The plan was to come upon the Carthaginians by surprise, to take Carthage as soon as possible after landing, and to force the government to accept the conditions dictated by Rome. The attempt nearly succeeded. The army, commanded by M. Atilius Regulus, disembarked safely, ravaged a large part of the Carthaginian territory, and advanced right up to the city. But the city held out against Regulus. His army was too small to take it; and the Romans, occupied with the fighting in Sicily and aware that Carthage still possessed a strong fleet, were afraid that, if they sent reinforcements, their whole enterprise might be ruined. With the aid of Xanthippus, an experienced Spartan general whom they invited to Africa with a body of mercenaries, the Carthaginians defeated the army of Regulus, and only a few survivors were able to sail back to Sicily.

Sicily now became once more the sole theatre of war. Here, too, Rome displayed the same stubbornness and persistence as in her Italian campaigns. Towards the end of this war there were times when she suffered defeat after defeat. At one time she had hardly any fleet left: several squadrons, one after another, were driven by storms to destruction on the coast of Sicily. But no disaster could weaken the resolution of Rome; and she was encouraged by the failure of Carthage to take advantage of these disasters. At last this stubbornness, together with the excellent quality of the Roman infantry, proved victorious. By degrees the Carthaginian armies were forced back into the south-west corner of Sicily, in spite of stubborn resistance, which was led, towards the end of the war, by Hamilcar Barca, a young Carthaginian general. The last phase of the war exhausted the strength of both combatants so completely that Rome consented to conditions of peace which were comparatively lenient to her rival. Carthage was forced to pay a moderate sum of money and to forfeit to Rome her Sicilian possessions. The first Roman 'province' was thus acquired.

Carthage Begins to Exploit Spain

After the conclusion of peace, Carthage had to undergo further trials and dangers. A body of mercenaries who had served in Sicily, enraged by the retention of their pay, mutinied on their return to Africa. Ruined by taxes and exhausted by drafts, the Berbers, some Numidians, and even some Phoenician cities on the coast, joined the mutineers. The position was critical. But Carthage showed in the hour of danger how much vital power she still possessed. Hamilcar Barca, the able young general mentioned above, to whom Carthage owed the favourable conditions of peace, crushed the revolt and restored order in the Carthaginian Empire; indeed, by a series of successful campaigns he extended the Carthaginian sphere of influence in Numidia.

After the war with the mercenaries the next task of Carthage was to restore the shattered resources of the state. Her markets in Italy and Gaul, her provinces of Sicily, Sardinia, and Corsica, were lost beyond recall; the two last were annexed by Rome after the conclusion of peace, and their loss was especially grievous, as these islands were not only the granaries of Carthage but also furnished copper and iron with other metals. The necessity of repairing this twofold loss explains the efforts of Carthage to extend her possessions in Spain, a land fabulously rich, according to ancient standards, in minerals. Spain might also, if properly cultivated, take the place of Sardinia and Sicily as a producer of grain. Operations in Spain were not hindered by the Romans, whose present object was to force the Carthaginians to pay up the whole sum of money required of them.

The task of creating a Spanish province, entrusted to Hamilcar Barca, was bequeathed by him to his son-in-law Hasdrubal, and later to his son Hannibal. There is no doubt that Hamilcar and his successors were led on by the hope of revenge as well as by economic considerations. They reckoned on turning Spain not only to a source of wealth but also to a weapon of war. The people had long been famous for their warlike spirit; and the country, by reason of its mineral wealth, was eminently suitable for the creation of extensive arsenals, and might prove an excellent base for a campaign against Rome. By degrees what had been small trading factories were converted into large seaport towns with considerable territories; one such town was Gades, the modern Cadiz. The Spanish tribes, one after another, some by force of arms and others by diplomatic means, became allies and tributaries of Carthage; and thus the Carthaginian base in Spain became steadily stronger and more extensive.

The Second Punic War Rocks the Known World

Michael Grant

Perhaps the single most dramatic episode in Rome's rise to Mediterranean dominance was the Second Punic War, fought between Rome and Carthage from 218 to 201 B.C. It was not only the largest, most costly war in human history up to that time, but also the first conflict having enough of an international dimension to be called a world war. In this masterful summary of the conflict, noted University of Edinburgh scholar Michael Grant calls it "the most momentous war of all time," with the exception of the conflicts of the twentieth century. This was because the second defeat of Carthage won Rome control of the entire western Mediterranean sphere and opened the way for further Roman expansion across the breadth of the known world. Grant covers the immediate causes of the war; the initial spectacular victories of Carthage's gifted general, Hannibal; Hannibal's failed attempt to induce Rome's Italian allies to defect to him; Roman victories in Spain; and the Roman general Scipio's climactic invasion of Africa.

The gravest menace to Italy in the 220s B.C. . . . came from the armies [the Carthaginians] maintained in Spain. Their dominant position in that peninsula was a new phenomenon, or rather the revival of an old one, for Carthage had earlier possessed a Spanish coastal empire. During the middle years of the third century B.C., when it lost the First Punic War and was expelled from Sicily and Sardinia and Corsica, it had also, under pressure from Greek Massilia (Marseille) which competed for the western Mediterranean ports, been deprived of almost the whole of its former Spanish dominions until finally little more than Gades (Cádiz) and the Straits of Gibraltar remained in its hands. But after putting an end to the ferocious mercenary revolt [directly following the First Punic War], the Carthaginians achieved a startling revival and, employing their subject lands in Algeria and Morocco as stepping stones, soon proceeded to build up a Spanish empire all over again. The agents of this recovery were the most able family Carthage ever produced, the house of the Barcids. In spite of determined political opponents, they had gained an impressive position at home, and now they settled themselves for several decades in Spain, establishing a hereditary line of semi-independent governors.

The Events Leading to War

The first of the family to set himself up there was Hamilcar Barca, who had played a distinguished part in the First Punic War, when he earned substantial credit for the resistance that postponed his side's defeat. Next, when the war was over, and when he had again fulfilled a leading role in the suppression of the rebellious mercenaries, he was authorized by his government in 237 B.C. to proceed to Spanish waters; his task was to recapture territories and resources in compensation for the loss of Sicily and the other islands. His successes in Spain were impressive. Starting from Gades, he reconquered most of the southern and eastern regions of the country as far north as Cape Ifach and Cape Nao, halfway up the coast; and near the limits of this occupation, beside lands that recalled the most fertile territories of north Africa, he established a port and capital at Acra Leuce, the White Promontory (Alicante). Already the Spanish territories he had occupied were larger and richer than those the Carthaginians had ruled before; and the Spaniards, men of mixed Celtic and Iberian stock famous for their physical endurance, provided him with a new army—the best Carthage had ever possessed throughout its history. The finely tempered Celtic swords that these soldiers carried were products of the immensely rich mines the conquests included. A share in the revenues from these mines went to Hamilcar's political enemies at Carthage and induced them not to obstruct him.

In 229, however, he was drowned. His son-in-law Hasdrubal, who succeeded him, moved his headquarters further south, in order to be near his home base. The site he chose, Carthago Nova or New Carthage (Cartagena), stood on a peninsula commanding one of the best harbors in the world; and it was protected from the interior by a lagoon, though a valley provided access to the abundant silver mines its townsmen exploited. Yet although Hasdrubal had selected this more southerly capital, he pushed the frontier of the new Carthaginian Spain a long way to the north, advancing to the banks of the River Iberus (Ebro), halfway up to the Pyrenees. And he also expanded his conquests deep into the interior, arranging a coordinated series of alliances and treaties, such as the Greeks who had settled in the same country had never succeeded in achieving.

Then Hasdrubal was murdered (221) and the command passed to his brother-in-law Hannibal, the son of Hamilcar Barca who had originally brought him out to Spain. Hannibal pushed still further inland as far as the River Douro and beyond the Tagus; and his diplomatic methods earned him considerable popularity among the Spaniards. However, one coastal town south of the Ebro, Saguntum (Sagunto), decided to resist him. With the Romans, on the other hand, this place was more friendly, and indeed, under the direction of an anti-Carthaginian party, it may have formed some sort of alliance with them. At all events, it was to Rome that the Saguntines now appealed—perhaps not for the first time. And Rome, its war party led by the Aemilii and Scipios, took the fateful step of responding favorably. Before long its delegates were on their way to Hannibal at Carthago Nova in order to transmit the Senate's command that he should keep his hands off Saguntum. A peace party at Carthage was in favor of complying, but Hannibal rejected the ultimatum and pressed on with the blockade of Saguntum, which fell to him (219) after a savage eight months' siege. The Romans angrily ordered the Carthaginian government to hand Hannibal over to them—a demand that was predictably turned down. Debate in the Senate about what should be done next was keen and bitter; but finally the Roman envoy told the Carthaginians that their refusal to surrender Hannibal meant war. The curtain was now going up for the most terrible of all Rome's struggles and the most far-reaching in its results—the Second Punic War (218).

Hannibal's Initial Victories

The real, underlying motive of the Romans' action, as so often in their subsequent history, was a profound suspicion of the foreigner—in this case, of Hasdrubal's successor Hannibal, whom they suspected of planning a major campaign across the Ebro. As to his own attitude, he must have known that his siege of Saguntum, whether it violated a formal Carthaginian treaty with the Romans or not, involved a serious risk of war against them. The legend, which may be true, was that his father had once made him swear eternal hatred towards the Romans. But, in any case, he evidently felt determined to avenge his country's defeat in the First Punic War, and Rome's perfidious behavior after it had ended. And he believed that the new Spanish empire his family had won, rich in minerals and warriors, gave him his opportunity to carry out these plans of vengeance and reversal.

But the Romans, too, were confident in their human resources, and so now they declared war. They intended to send forces to Spain via the land route and Massilia and to send them to the north African homeland of Carthage as well.

However, both these designs were forestalled by Hannibal's audacious decision to invade Italy. This came as a surprise to Rome, which knew he had constructed no fleet. But instead he made for Italy by the difficult land route. He took with him, on the final stage of the march, some forty thousand men, comprising well-trained, Carthaginian-officered Spanish infantry and excellent African (Numidian) cavalry, with thirty-seven elephants. And he confidently hoped to augment this army on arrival in north Italy by winning over anti-Roman Gauls and Rome's Italian subject allies; in this way he would be able to cut off the vast reservoir of Roman-Italian manpower before it could ever be drawn upon.

In April 218 B.C., brushing aside native opposition, he

transferred his army across the Rhone [River, in what is now southern France], and then in the early autumn he crossed the Alps. The mountains were treacherous going because of premature falls of snow, but Rome's belief that they would stop an army from getting through proved mistaken. Nevertheless, when Hannibal came down into the Po valley, he had only twenty-six thousand men left, and the Senate's generals hoped to wear him down by a series of delaying actions. But they were almost at once defeated in two successive battles, on a northern and then a southern tributary of the Po. First, on the River Ticinus (Ticino), where they tried to engage Hannibal's tired army before it could recover, a skirmish between advance guards displayed his cavalry's superior speed, equipment, and training so clearly that the Romans fell back across the river to the Apennine foothills. There, on a rough, snowy December day their commanders, instead of staying on the higher ground as they should have done, were induced by a feigned Carthaginian flight to order their forty thousand legionaries to wade across the swollen waters of the River Trebia (Trebbia), and attack him. But the morale of the Roman soldiers was low because they had had no breakfast, and in the morning mist an ambush from the reed beds took them by surprise in flank and rear, so that they were overwhelmed and only a quarter of their numbers escaped the subsequent massacre.

Why Hannibal Chose Not to Besiege Rome

And so already, within only two months, Hannibal had overrun the whole of northern Italy, with the isolated exception of two newly founded Latin colonies at Placentia (Piacenza) and Cremona, which stood firm. It was true that he had lost most of his elephants; and the help he received from the local Gauls was not all he had hoped for. Yet as a result of his victories, he was able to increase his force to a total strength of fifty thousand. And now, from his new north Italian base, he believed the time had come to incite Rome's Italian allies to revolt. Meanwhile at Rome itself, the more prosperous among the plebeians, who controlled their own Council and the National Assembly, were infuriated by the bungling that had lost them the north Italian lands they had fought so hard to win; and their appointment of the reformist "new man" Flaminius to a second consulship in 217 was a criticism of the Senate's conduct of the war.

Flaminius tried to block the Carthaginian army's southward advance, but early in the year they evaded him by breaking through an unguarded Apennine pass; and then they pressed on through marshy country, in such rough conditions that Hannibal, riding on the sole surviving elephant, lost the sight of an eye through exposure to the icy cold. However, as he ravaged Etruria and seemed to be making for Rome, he drew Flaminius after him and on a foggy April morning trapped his army in a defile between the hills and Lake Trasimene. Surrounded on all three sides, most of the soldiers of two Roman legions were killed, and Flaminius himself was among the fallen. This victory presented Hannibal with an open, undefended road to Rome itself. However, he did not take the opportunity. This was partly because the total destruction of Roman power might not have been in his own country's interests, for it would only have introduced rival powers from the eastern Mediterranean to fill the vacuum. But in any case, he lacked good siege equipment; and in its absence, the walls of Rome could not be breached by any attacker, especially without a supply base nearby. And no such base existed because, to Hannibal's acute disappointment, not one single town of central Italy defected to his side. Rome's system of colonies and allies stood this searching test with admirable firmness.

So Hannibal swerved aside from the city and instead decided to seek allies in the southern part of the peninsula, which, for the most part, was non-Italian and un-Romanized. As he marched through Campania and Apulia, relying on their grainlands for food and on their ports for contact with Carthage, his army was shadowed by a veteran Roman general, Fabius Maximus, now dictator. Fabius's reappointment had been arranged, with the concurrence of the Senate, by the unusual procedure of election in the Assembly, since one of the consuls who should have nominated him was dead and the other was cut off from the city. Fabius was a Roman of the old and canny type, and the strategy he now put into effect avoided risking his hastily recruited new armies in any further pitched battles—a policy that earned him the nickname of Cunctator (Delayer)—while instead he cut off the enemy's supplies by devastating the surrounding countryside. But this policy of caution and destruction was understandably hated by many Romans and Italians and lost him the popular support that had brought him to power.

Rome Suffers Disaster, Then Rebounds

In the following year, therefore, the generalship was removed from him and bestowed on two inexperienced consuls, who were entrusted with the largest army Rome had ever put into the field; they were placed in joint command of the force as consuls had never been before, since it had hitherto been the custom for each to command his own separate army. In a supreme effort to end the war at a single blow, they accepted battle on a smooth open plain near Cannae, a small fortress near Italy's heel. Hannibal had provoked them to this by seizing the place, which contained a valuable depot of stores; and then he chose an open plain for the battle to show the Romans they had nothing to fear from reserves. Believing that their numerical superiority would tell, they attacked, and Hannibal allowed his convex crescent or échelon to become concave under the pressure of their center. But the prevailing hot sirocco wind blew blinding clouds of sand into the faces of the Romans, and they found themselves caught in a pincer movement by the enemy's light troops on either flank and cavalry in the rear. Wedged tight in these hopeless conditions, the Roman army, after savage resistance, was almost wholly destroyed. This battle, the bloodiest defeat Rome ever suffered, provided an unprecedented example of a smaller force successfully enveloping a larger one on both sides, a tactic that required perfect coordination and was admired by the German general von Schlieffen and studied in the First World War in 1914.

One of the consuls was killed in action, but the other, although a nominee of the Assembly and consequently blamed for everything by later conservative historians, received a courteous reception at Rome from his fellow senators who thanked him for not despairing of the republic—for in the city, despite this catastrophe, morale remained indomitable. Indeed, even before the end of the very same year, under a government now unquestioningly left in the hands of the Senate, Rome's terrible losses were already more than made good by further recruitment, so that Hannibal's victory had failed to repair his numerical disadvantage. Moreover, in order to avert further disastrous pitched battles, Fabius's strategy was seen to have been good after all, and was revived; the Roman armies were divided into a number of small forces distributed at vital points, like a pack of dogs circling around a lion. Yet Cannae had led, at last, to some of the defections Rome had feared—not, indeed, among its subject allies in the center of the peninsula, but in the geographically remoter and culturally more alien areas of south Italy and Sicily, where the vitally important cities of Capua, Syracuse, and Tarentum all successively went over to the invader (216–213). These desertions, and above all the defection of Capua, gave Hannibal sorely needed men, weapons, bases, and supplies. Nevertheless, by a series of mighty sieges, conducted by double cordons of troops supplied with the most scientific equipment, all the rebellious towns were gradually won back again, Capua and Syracuse in 211, and Tarentum in 209.

In 213 or 212, despite all these troubles, Rome emphasized its status as a major power by issuing for the first time, on a large scale, its historic silver coin the *denarius* which provided a much improved means of meeting the state's financial needs. Nor was it of any avail, in 211, for Hannibal to advance to the outskirts of Rome itself. Accompanied by an escort of cavalry, he rode slowly around the walls on his black horse, watched by the inhabitants on the walls. At that very moment, as it happened, the site of his camp, three miles away, came up for auction in the city—and was duly sold at a normal price. Nothing could have shown him more clearly that the Romans, in spite of all the disasters they had suffered at his hands, were still determined to survive and win.

The Roman Offensive in Spain

Because of the remarkable dramas of Hannibal's Italian invasion, the Second Punic War is often looked at as a war fought primarily on Italian soil, with a secondary sphere of operations in Spain. But the Spanish campaigns fought during the same years were a deciding factor in the outcome of the war. Although the Romans had failed to keep Hannibal from crossing the Pyrenees and marching on Italy, they nevertheless succeeded in preventing his younger brother Hasdrubal Barca, whom he had left behind to rule Carthage's Spanish empire, from sending him any reinforcements. This they did by making the fateful decision to fight an active war in Spain itself, despite all the crises that they were undergoing in their homeland.

Rome's Spanish armies were commanded, for the first seven years of the war, by two men named Scipio, the father and uncle of the great Scipio Africanus. In spite of initial offensives by Hasdrubal Barca, the Scipios gained a number of successes that enabled them to gain control of the Mediterranean seaboard of the country, moving gradually southwards along its coast until in 211 they captured Saguntum, the original bone of contention, which they then made preparations to use as a base for further advances. Because of these setbacks Hasdrubal Barca failed on several occasions in attempts to break out across the Pyrenees. Moreover, successive drafts of recruits, who would have been very useful to Hannibal's Italian campaigns, had to be diverted from north Africa to his brother's Spanish army instead. Yet the diversion of these troops, which gave such an invaluable breathing space to the hard-pressed Romans in Italy, caused the downfall of the Scipios in Spain, for in 211 both the brothers were successively defeated and died in battle.

The Carthaginians were now able to take back the regions they had lost south of the Ebro. Yet they did not cross the river. After their losses of Capua and Syracuse in the same year, they did not feel confident enough to tackle the defenses, somewhat feeble though they were, that the Roman survivors of the Scipios' defeats had erected along its banks. Moreover, as soon became clear, Rome had by no means finished with Spain. In 210 the Assembly, at last reemerging from the timidity imposed by its earlier failures against Hannibal, induced the Senate to acquiesce in the appointment of a new and surprising general to command the Spanish armies. This was Publius Cornelius Scipio (later Africanus), son and nephew of the commanders who had perished in Spain the year before. Publius Scipio was only twenty-five. He had therefore held none of the senior offices regarded as necessary prerequisites for such an appointment. Yet he was not untried in war, and his exploits had inspired the conviction that he was the right man for the job.

Scipio Wins Spain

Once in Spain, he reverted to the attacking strategy of his father and uncle. He chose as his target the enemy headquarters and arsenal at Carthago Nova. While assaulting the town from the land side, he profited by a squall, which had blown up and lowered the level of the lagoon, to send his troops through the shallow waters and scale the fortifications that were undefended on this side—and by this means the whole of Carthago Nova fell into his hands (209). In the following year, he marched into the interior of the country and engaged Hasdrubal Barca's smaller army at Baecula (Bailén) on the upper Baetis (Guadalquivir). Compelled to fight quickly because he feared the arrival of enemy reinforcements, Scipio divided up his main force and, using his light troops as a screen, fell on the enemy's flanks. This striking demonstration of a novel flexibility in Roman tactics, which showed how carefully Scipio had studied Hannibal's Italian victories, won him the battle.

Yet Hasdrubal Barca escaped and at last got out of Spain altogether, taking an unexpected land route around the western extremity of the Pyrenees and proceeding onwards to Italy, with the intention of joining his brother Hannibal there. His escape transformed the battle of Baecula from a tactical victory into a strategic defeat. And Scipio did not try to pursue him. Probably his orders from Rome did not allow him to; but even if they did, he was right not to make the attempt—since, if he had done so, he would have exposed himself in difficult country too far from his base and would thus have risked losing Spain altogether; and besides, he would never have caught Hasdrubal Barca in any case. As it was, the departure of Hasdrubal Barca's army insured final Roman success in the Spanish campaign. This was sealed by a huge battle in 206 against his successors, fought at Ilipa (Alcala del Rio, near Seville). Here Scipio introduced a sophisticated variation into his outflanking tactics by reversing the usual battle order and moving his light auxiliaries from the flanks to the center of his line. This meant that the men now located on the flanks were his best troops, the legionaries; it was they who now found themselves entrusted with the encirclement of the enemy force, and they carried out their task triumphantly. This time, the victory was conclusive. Many native princes abandoned their alliances with Carthage. And by the end of the year, it had lost its Spanish possessions forever.

And so these most valuable portions of the Iberian peninsula had fallen into the hands of Rome, which annexed them and converted them into two new provinces: the eastern coastal strip of Nearer Spain, and beyond it, Further Spain (Baetica) comprising the southern coast and the valley of the Baetis (Guadalquivir). Eight years later, the Roman government appointed two new praetors to administer these territories. A five percent tribute was imposed on grain, resembling the taxes earlier instituted in Sicily. But otherwise, the pattern was different, for it seemed practicable in this more warlike country to add the duty of military service, so that the country's manpower resources could provide auxiliary units to supplement the legions. Moreover, the Romans developed and expanded Carthaginian mining in the country, which was rightly said to overflow with metals; at Carthago Nova alone, the capital of the Nearer Province, the silver mines subsequently employed as many as forty thousand workers at one time. And so a fixed sum in silver was levied on the population in addition to the tribute. . . .

Hannibal's Brother Is Defeated

[Meanwhile] the removal of Hasdrubal Barca's army from Spain was Hannibal's gain in Italy. And it came at a very appropriate time. For in spite of their successes in south Italy, the Romans were almost at the end of their resources. In 209, twelve Latin colonies out of the existing thirty had declared their inability to supply any more troops, or the money to pay for them. They had been bled white and could fight no more. Moreover, Etruscan cities, too, were beginning to be disaffected. And now the arrival of Hasdrubal, fulfilling hopes that Carthage had been cherishing for eleven years, caused alarm throughout Italy. After crossing southern France and the Alps unopposed, he descended into the Po valley, where new Gaulish recruits raised his numbers to thirty thousand. Then the two Carthaginian brothers moved towards one another, intending to join forces.

Meanwhile the Romans, after mobilizing massively yet again, and in spite of their exhaustion, had an army in the north of Italy and an army in the south. At this juncture they benefited from a great stroke of luck: captured dispatch riders of Hasdrubal revealed to them that his meeting place with Hannibal was to be in Umbrian territory. On receiving this news, the southern Roman commander Gaius Claudius Nero, leaving a force to watch Hannibal, undertook a rapid six-day, two-hundred-and-forty-mile march up the Adriatic coast to the Umbrian river Metaurus (Metauro). On the following morning Hasdrubal heard a double bugle call from the camp of the Romans, which told him that their two armies had united. This meant that he was outnumbered by at least ten thousand men. In a desperate attempt to slip through and join forces with his brother, he moved up the Metaurus valley after nightfall. But he lost his way in the dark and was overtaken among the gorges and slippery crags, and died fighting—and almost all his men died with him.

For the first time during the entire long period of the war, the Romans had won a pitched battle in their homeland, and the end of Hannibal's occupation of Italy was now only a matter of time. He learned what had happened when his brother's head was hurled into his camp. Then he withdrew into the mountains of Italy's toe and stayed there, without emerging, for another four years.

When two of these years had passed (205), Scipio, fresh

from his Spanish victories, was elected consul and asked the Senate for permission to invade Africa and attack Carthage directly. The senators were very reluctant, since they still felt apprehensive of Hannibal's continued presence in Italy and were anxious not to impose further burdens on the allied towns. But when Scipio appealed over their heads to the Assembly, promising vengeance on the Carthaginians for all the sufferings they had inflicted, the Senate gave way, somewhat grudgingly. That is to say, it agreed that, whereas Sicily was to be his province, he could also sail to Africa if the interests of the state required it, with two legions in addition to whatever volunteers he could collect. He recruited seven thousand of them, thus bringing his total army up to thirty thousand, and with this force landed in north Africa some twenty miles from Carthage (204). There he was joined by a neighboring prince Masinissa, ruler of part of Numidia (eastern Algeria), who had changed sides along with his excellent cavalry.

Rome's Total Victory

In the next year Hannibal returned from Italy, his fifteen-year-long invasion at an end. His early victories in Italy had temporarily silenced his political opponents at home. After the loss of Capua, however, they had begun to be much more vociferous [loudly vocal]. And now, finally, Carthage had begun negotiations for peace with the Romans and the discussions had reached an advanced stage. Nevertheless, Hannibal was still able to persuade his government to break these talks off. Thereupon Scipio moved inland to sever the enemy capital from its agricultural supplies, and in 202, near Zama, seventy-five miles from the city, the final battle of the war was fought. It was not a real climax because the eventual outcome of the campaign could be in no doubt. But it achieved great fame owing to the caliber of the rival commanders—and before the engagement, the two men had a famous meeting about which nothing is known, except that it was unproductive.

When the battle began, neither side succeeded in outflanking the other, for both were by now thoroughly familiar with tactics of this kind. But the issue was decided by the horsemen of Rome's new Numidian allies, who broke off their pursuit of the enemy's cavalry wings and fell on their rear, achieving total victory. There were few Carthaginian survivors, but Hannibal was one of them. He recommended to his government that peace should be made immediately, and this was done. The terms were less favorable than they would have been in the previous year if negotiations had not been suspended. The indemnity to be paid by the Carthaginians was doubled; their fleet was limited to ten ships instead of twenty; and Masinissa, who became king of all Numidia, was rewarded with part of their western borderlands. And finally, they were forbidden, henceforward, to engage in any war without the prior consent of Rome.

They had already lost Spain, and now they had ceased to be a major power and would never become one again. So the Romans had victoriously completed the most decisive single phase of their rise to domination. The Second Punic War had made it certain that they would remain in control of the entire western Mediterranean region for many hundreds of years to come. For the West, therefore, with the possible exception of the struggles of the twentieth century A.D., the Second Punic War proved to have been the most momentous war of all time.

But victory had only been won by feats of unprecedented endurance. In spite of initial disastrous defeats, the Italian dominion built up with such patience by Rome had, on the whole, resisted the temptation to defect, fully justifying the Roman system. Even in the gravest peril Roman and Italian morale and discipline had stood firm, leaving memories of this supreme test which later writers were never tired of recalling. The solid virtues of many Romans and Italians, working together as loyal, obedient partners within a tradition built up over many generations, had prevailed and won the day.

Rome's Worst Defeat:
The Battle of Cannae

Brian Caven

In examining Rome's rise to greatness, it is clear that its successes and gains far outweighed its failures and losses. Yet it would be a mistake to ignore those failures and losses, for on more than one occasion they brought the Roman state nearly to brink of collapse. The most obvious and dramatic example is one of the battles of the Second Punic War, at Cannae, in southeastern Italy. There, the wily and resourceful Hannibal delivered the Romans their worst battlefield defeat ever. Rome's total casualties may have numbered more than 50,000, including one of the two consuls and some eighty senators. In this essay, from his detailed book about the Punic Wars, scholar Brian Caven describes the immediate events leading up to the battle, the size and deployment of the forces (including speculation about what the Roman plan may have been), the engagement itself, in which Hannibal sprung a huge trap on the unsuspecting Romans, and the aftermath. Caven regularly cites the accounts of these events by the second-century B.C. Greek historian Polybius and the first-century B.C. Roman historian Livy.

In the winter of 217/16 no cautious betting man would have offered any but the longest odds against Hannibal's ultimate victory. He had indeed won two battles and was at present wintering securely in Apulia, but he had not brought about the defection of a single Roman ally or taken a single important town. It is true that a measure of disaffection was growing both in southern Italy—the region most recently incorpo-

Excerpted from *The Punic Wars*, by Brian Caven (New York: Marboro Books, 1992). Copyright © 1980 by Brian Caven. Reprinted by permission of Palgrave.

rated into the confederation—and in Campania [the fertile region of southwest Italy containing Capua and Pompeii], where there were social and political grievances; but Hannibal would have to do better than he had done so far if these sentiments were to lead to open revolt. The Romans had latterly held their own in Apulia, Carthage had made no serious effort to dispute their command of the sea, Hannibal had been losing men and horses without any means of replacing them, and the news from Spain was extremely encouraging. . . .

Senate and people were fully alive to the very real danger, to say nothing of the disgrace, of allowing Hannibal to ravage the lands of their allies with impunity. . . .

[Nevertheless] the consuls of 217 BC had been 'advised' by the Senate to avoid a general action with Hannibal in the spring, prior to handing over their armies to their successors. However in the clashes that occurred between their forces and Hannibal's foragers the Romans more than held their own. Accordingly in early June, with his supplies running out, Hannibal left Gerunium, marched the sixty miles across the Tavoliere and seized the small abandoned town of Cannae, which stands upon an abrupt rocky eminence not far from the right bank of the Aufidus (Ofanto) roughly midway between the important city of Canusium (Canosa) and the sea and which the local inhabitants had been using as a granary. . . . With Cannae as his supply base Hannibal began to plunder the plain of the Aufidus, a country that was suitable for the employment of cavalry.

The Opposing Armies Camp Near Each Other

The narrative of Polybius—although not that of Livy—suggests, probably rightly, that the proconsuls had followed Hannibal part of the way to Cannae. They wrote repeatedly to the consuls and Senate asking for instructions, pointing out that they could not approach his camp without being obliged to attempt to check his depredations [destructive acts] and that they could not do that without accepting battle. They were ordered to wait for the arrival of their successors and [the new consuls] Varro and Paullus, having done what needed to be done at Rome, set off for the front with their levies, armed with the Senate's authorization to offer battle to the enemy. When they reached the camps they sent Regulus back to Rome on the grounds of his age and then marched directly across the plain to a point about six miles to the north-west of where Hannibal lay, and camped there. . . . Paullus wanted to fight on ground of his own choosing—ground less favourable to cavalry—which would have involved pressing on to the south where the country rises slightly. However the consuls, when they began their march, can scarcely have been ignorant of Hannibal's position, which was probably between the hill of Cannae and the river. . . .

On the day following their arrival—it was now the end of July—Varro, the commander of the day, moved the army towards the river, below Cannae. Hannibal attacked him on the march with his horsemen and light infantry, but Varro deployed some of his heavy infantry in support of his skirmishers and cavalry and the Carthaginians were driven off. The next day Paullus fortified a camp on the left bank of the river and threw a third of his forces across to occupy a smaller camp, a little over a mile higher up and about a mile and a half from the camp of Hannibal. From this position the Romans could cover the foraging parties from their main camp and harass those of the enemy. Hannibal countered this move by transferring his own forces to the left bank of the river, thus proclaiming his readiness to fight. Throughout his whole campaign he had attached so much importance to intelligence that we may be sure that he knew as much as he needed to know about the consuls and the current temper of Senate and people. He knew, in short, that the Romans had come to Cannae in order to fight. He had had plenty of time to make up his mind where he intended the battle to take place; the 'how' he left open until he saw what tactics the enemy proposed to adopt.

Two days after crossing the river Hannibal offered battle but Paullus, whose day it was, refused—why, it is impossible to say. Hannibal therefore sent the Numidians to harass the smaller Roman camp and prevent the men from watering; a move which produced precisely the reaction on the part of the enemy that he had hoped for. Next day, 2 August, Varro marched out his men at daybreak from both camps and drew them up on the right bank of the Aufidus. He was accepting the challenge that his colleague had refused.

The Size and Deployment of the Forces

Varro intended to apply the lessons of the Trebia. There the legions had crushed the Punic centre but had been prevented from exploiting their success by the rout of their wings by the elephants and cavalry. At Cannae there were no elephants to fear; but as Hannibal drew up his army his best troops formed the wings of his infantry and therefore the wings constituted the dangerous areas. The answer, as Varro saw it, was to have no wings—to mass all the heavy infantry in the centre, punch a hole a thousand yards wide in the middle of Hannibal's line, re-form and then—this is quite conjectural—hold off one of the isolated Punic wings with a part of his infantry and throw the rest with overwhelming weight of numbers against the other and annihilate it. The rôle of the cavalry was to protect the flanks and rear of the phalanx during its advance. For he was, in effect, going to sacrifice the flexibility of the manipular formation to the solidity and weight of the phalanx. To ensure that the Roman and allied horse, outnumbered and outclassed by the enemy, fought with the necessary spirit and determination the consuls themselves would lead them, leaving the command of the infantry to the proconsul Servilius.

Accordingly Varro drew up his infantry in mass formation, narrowing the gaps between the maniples, reducing their fronts, and deepening them correspondingly. The Roman cavalry under Paullus were stationed on the right flank of the infantry, with their own right flank protected by the river, which in those days was still flowing in early August although today its bed is at that season quite dry. The left flank of the infantry was covered by Varro himself with the allied horse.

Polybius tells us that 6,000 cavalry took part in the battle on the Roman side; but then he, as well as Livy, also believed that the Romans had eight legions, and not four, in the line.

Battle of Cannae

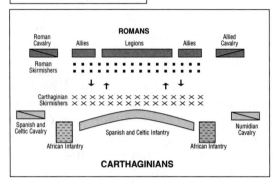

Stage 1. As the opposing armies prepare for battle, the Romans form ranks in their usual fashion, with their strongest infantry—made up of Roman legionaries—in the center, flanked by their allied infantry, and on the wings the Roman and allied cavalry units. Aware that the Romans mean to aim for his own center and overwhelm it, Hannibal moves his strongest infantry—the Africans—back to holding positions on the flanks and draws up his less formidable Spanish and Celtic infantry units in a crescent formation in the center. The battle opens with a clash of the light-armed skirmishers of the opposing sides.

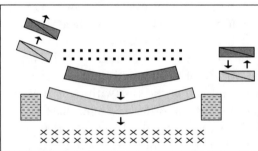

Stage 2. After the initial, indecisive exchange between the skirmishers, per the usual procedure they retreat to the rear and the opposing infantry units advance on each other. The Roman legions and allied units push the weaker Carthaginian center backward, just as Hannibal had anticipated they would, while he shrewdly continues to hold his Africans in reserve. Mean-while, the cavalry units on the right clash, while on the left the Roman cavalry breaks and flees from the numerically superior Spanish and Celtic cavalry.

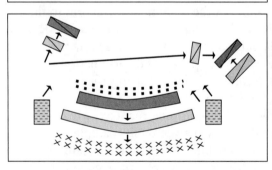

Stage 3. As the Roman infantrymen continue to press forward believing they are winning the battle, Hannibal's brilliant trap begins to spring on them. With the added support of his skirmishers in the rear, his center holds. At the same time, his Africans turn toward the center and begin to envelop the Roman flanks. Meanwhile, as a small contingent of his Spanish and Celtic cavalry pursues the Roman horsemen off the field, the rest swing behind the Roman army and attack the Roman allied cavalry from the rear.

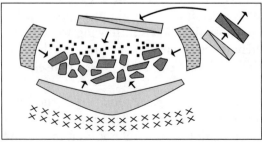

Stage 4. Assaulted front and back by the enemy, the Roman allied cavalry breaks and flees, pursued by Hannibal's Numidians. His Spanish and Celtic cavalry then wheels around and attacks the Roman center from behind. Now nearly surrounded, the normally disciplined Roman ranks fall apart and a massive slaughter ensues. Some 50,000 Romans are killed, the largest single battlefield loss in Rome's history, while Hannibal, whose victory is complete, loses only 6,000 to 7,000 men.

However, since this figure of 6,000 horse does not fit the normal ratios of citizen cavalry to foot soldiers (300 to an over-strength legion) and of allied cavalry to citizen (three to one) . . . it may represent the true number and not one deduced by the historian. On the other hand it may be the result of guesswork on the part of Polybius' Punic sources, and the Romans may have had no more than 1,200 citizen, and 3,600—or even, if we follow Livy, only 2,400—allied horse on the field. After all, the confederation had suffered serious losses in cavalry during the previous year. The skirmishers, who must have numbered about 10,000, were thrown forward to cover the whole front.

Hannibal led his men back across the river, and behind a screen of light infantry drew up his army in order of battle. The Spanish and Gallic cavalry under Hasdrubal faced the Roman knights; the Numidians under Hanno faced the allied horse. The two wings of his infantry were formed by the Africans, the cream of his foot soldiers, now armed in the Roman manner, while the Spanish and Gallic swordsmen, in alternate companies, comprised the centre; the naked torsos and the golden torques and armlets of the Celts contrasting strikingly with the purple-bordered linen tunics of the Iberians. The centre was the thinnest part of the line and was drawn up so as to form a fairly deep crescent-shaped bulge towards the enemy. Hannibal himself and his brother Mago commanded the infantry, and the course of the battle suggests that they took their stance on the wings among the Africans. . . . Hannibal must have had about 30,000 infantry in the line, apart from the light-armed, and the Romans must have had much the same number; but in cavalry Hannibal with some 10,000 horsemen enjoyed a decided advantage.

Hannibal Springs His Giant Trap

The battle commenced with the usual clash between the light forces on both sides that preceded the arrival on the scene of the heavy infantry and cavalry. On the Roman right the Roman knights, heavily outnumbered, were almost annihilated in a desperate dismounted engagement and the survivors were driven from the field, apart from a few who, like Paullus himself, attached themselves to the infantry in order to continue the fight. On their left the bridleless Numidians were content by attacking, retreating and attacking again to keep the allied horsemen occupied and to detach them from the flank of the infantry, which it was their business to protect.

However, it was in the centre that the battle was decided. The great mass of Roman heavy infantry crashed into the bulge in Hannibal's line and as the barbarians resisted with all the savage fury of their races the Roman front adjusted itself to the convex face of the enemy line. Slowly, stabbing and slashing, the Iberians and Celts fell back, the Punic front straightened, caved in, collapsed, and the whole body of Roman infantry, jammed into the space between one horn of the now reversed crescent and the other, pressed forward in pursuit. Another—but this time a successful—breakthrough, such as had been achieved on the Trebia, seemed imminent. Then the trap, the more deadly and unexpected from having been set and baited before the eyes of the whole army, was sprung. Hannibal's wings, the crack African heavy infantry, which had up till now been unengaged, entered the battle. Either the right and left wings turned left and right respectively, and then dressed ranks from the right and left, or else—less probably, in the light of the language of Polybius—they simply wheeled left and right. By this manoeuvre, executed with parade-ground coolness and efficiency in the heat of the battle, the Africans, probably about ten thousand in number, changed front and positioned themselves so as to be able to attack the flanks of the Roman infantry. In the meantime Hasdrubal had re-formed his bridled cavalry—in itself no small achievement—and ridden across the rear of the Roman advance to fall upon the allied cavalry on the Roman left and drive them from the field without striking a blow. Leaving their pursuit to the Numidians, he now returned to the centre of the field and fell upon the rear of the Roman infantry at several places simultaneously.

It was here . . . that the consul Paullus fell fighting. And indeed the battle now became a massacre as Hannibal and Mago rolled up the flanks of what ceased to be an army and degenerated into a mere mass of men, huddled between the two inexorably advancing phalanxes of Africans, with the Celts and Spaniards, rallied and thirsting for revenge, assailing what had been its front while Hasdrubal's horsemen attacked it from the rear.

It is quite impossible to arrive at an accurate figure for the Roman losses. Wounded, other than those lightly wounded, who were left upon the enemy's field must always be included among the dead. According to Livy, some 19,000 fugitives escaped from the shambles to the two camps and to the rock of Cannae; but of these all except 4,200 were killed or (the greater number) taken. 6,400 surrendered in the small camp on the evening of the same day, and a similar number on the next day in the main camp. In all about 14,500 men are reckoned by the Romans to have got away. Of these 10,000 escaped to Canusium (this figure includes the 4,200 who made their way there from the main camp), and 4,500 to Venusia—to which the consul Varro, carried away in the rout of his cavalry, also escaped with only 50 knights. . . . The official Punic figure for their own dead was 5,700, of whom 4,000 were Celts. The wounded, however, must have amounted to two or three times this number, and of these, if we take into account the season of the year when the battle was fought and the state of medical knowledge at that time, we may reasonably conjecture that a great many subsequently died or suffered permanent disablement.

The Lessons of the Battle

The year 216 constitutes the high-water mark of Hannibal's military career and Cannae his greatest battle. Even in the twentieth century it is cited as a classic. It has been suggested that the battles on the Trebia and in Spain near Ibera in the early summer of 216 were intended to anticipate Cannae, but failed to do so because the Romans broke through the Punic centre before the wings were able to encircle them. If that is so perhaps the basic battle plan was one that Hamilcar had taught to his sons. But it took the genius of Hannibal to perceive on the field of battle itself how Varro's massed infantry attack could be confined to the centre of the

Punic line and held there long enough for the wings to move in unimpeded on its flanks. Cannae illustrated once again the ability of the various parts of Hannibal's army to manoeuvre independently yet in conjunction with each other, when actually in contact with the enemy; an ability strikingly in contrast with the monolithic character of the Roman infantry and its powerlessness to respond to and counter the tactical moves of the enemy. It illustrated, too, the use that can be made, even in an infantry battle, of well-led cavalry . . . and the folly of surrendering the fringes of the battle to the enemy—although this was a mistake which the consuls did in fact try to avoid with the inferior cavalry forces at their disposal.

Cannae was in itself a major disaster for Rome. Few ancient states could have taken in their stride—or even recovered from—the loss of twenty thousand or more men in a single day; but on its own its effect would not have been so calamitous. It was, however, the culmination of a long series of disasters: the Ticinus, the Trebia (about 15,000 men lost), Trasimene (25,000 killed and captured), the rout of Servilius' cavalry (some 4,000 killed and taken) and now Cannae. In less than three full campaigns, including the fighting in Campania and Apulia, the confederation had lost well over seventy-five thousand men, a high proportion of whom were of the knightly class; and not only had it lost almost twelve per cent of its available strength, it had apparently made no impression on that of Hannibal, who had gone from victory to victory. The most serious damage done by Cannae was to the myth of Roman invincibility. Cannae had been a formal trial by combat between the Roman confederation and Hannibal and the outcome seemed to indicate that Rome could not contain the invader or defend her allies.

Rome Defeats a Defecting Ally

Robert B. Kebric

The increasing international dimension of Rome's wars and conquests in the third and second centuries B.C. is exemplified by the fact that in the Second Punic War the Romans fought not only the Carthaginians, but also some Greek cities and kingdoms, including the powerful Greek city-state of Syracuse, in eastern Sicily. The clash with Syracuse was also significant in that it showed how ruthless the Romans could be in punishing former allies who had defected to the enemy. The town of Capua had gone over to Hannibal in 216 B.C., for example, and four years later the Romans had recaptured it, deprived it of its political rights, and beheaded its leaders. When Syracuse defected in similar fashion, Rome sent one of its greatest generals, Marcellus, to deal with the situation. This episode is also famous because in besieging Syracuse Marcellus was confronted with the highly effective defenses designed by Archimedes, the greatest mathematician and inventor of ancient times. The following well-informed synopsis of these events is by noted classical scholar Robert B. Kebric, of the University of Louisville, who quotes liberally from the first-century B.C. Greek biographer Plutarch's *Life of Marcellus*.

With a Carthaginian victory appearing imminent, anti-Roman sentiment spread rapidly through hostile parts of Italy, and even some former allies expelled pro-Roman officials and declared for Hannibal. Foremost among these was the great Greek city of Syracuse in Sicily.

Syracuse had enjoyed a long history of friendship with Rome. Hiero II, the city's tyrant, had initially sided with

Carthage when the First Punic War began in 264 B.C., but he reversed his policy within a year and became a staunch Roman ally until his death forty-eight years later. The alliance proved mutually beneficial, and when the Second Punic War broke out in 218 B.C., there was no question where Syracuse's loyalty lay—as long as Hiero was alive. Even after the disaster at Cannae when it appeared Rome might be overwhelmed by Hannibal, Hiero did not flinch, but the impact of that defeat would soon have its effect.

Not everyone at Syracuse viewed Rome in the positive light Hiero did. Anti-Roman sentiments began to emerge after the old tyrant died in 215 B.C. The political maneuvering that followed his death resulted in a dramatic turn-about in loyalties. Syracuse was no longer the guardian of Roman interests in Sicily but a Carthaginian ally. If Rome could not retake Syracuse, all of Sicily would probably fall into Carthaginian hands, providing Hannibal with uninterrupted reinforcements and supplies from Africa as well as Spain. Also, other Mediterranean powers who were still hesitating to commit fully to one side or the other would no longer have any reason to wait.

The "Sword of Rome" Goes to Syracuse

The Roman siege of Syracuse was placed under the direction of M. Claudius Marcellus, Rome's most capable and experienced general. Popularly known as the "Sword of Rome" because of his success against Hannibal, Marcellus had a long and distinguished military record. A veteran of the First Punic War, he served the earliest of his five consulships (222 B.C.) fighting Gauls in the north of Italy, where he killed the Gallic chieftain, Viridomarus, in a personal duel—an incident so reminiscent of Rome's heroic past that a play was produced about it.

In the Second Punic War, Marcellus was the first Roman commander to enjoy a victory over Hannibal, defending the city of Nola (about 20 miles east of Naples) in Campania against his attack in 216 B.C. The military impact of his deed was not as important as the effect it had on Roman morale. With Cannae and other disasters still fresh, Marcellus was able to provide the first hope that Hannibal could be defeated.

As proconsul in 215 B.C., Marcellus again thwarted Hannibal at Nola, which resulted in what Plutarch claims were the first enemy desertions to the Romans. Marcellus' efforts won him a third consulship in 214 B.C.; and after fending off Hannibal's final attempt to take Nola, he moved to assist in the siege of Casilinum, a strategic Campanian city that had fallen into Carthaginian hands. Once that city was retaken (another encouraging victory for the Romans), Marcellus was assigned to Sicily.

In 214 B.C., Hiero's inept young grandson and successor was assassinated by pro-Romans while he was visiting the nearby city of Leontini. Subsequently, other members of the royal family were put to death at Syracuse, and attempts were made to realign the city with Rome. However, the violence led the Syracusans to return pro-Carthaginian leaders to power in the next elections. They also encouraged neighboring Leontini to revolt against Rome. Marcellus and his general, Appius Claudius, stormed and captured Leontini in 213 B.C., but the city's sack and the rumored atrocities associated with it resolved the Syracusans once and for all to side with Carthage. Marcellus and Appius now led a combined land and sea attack against Syracuse.

The Greatest Ancient Scientist

Syracuse was the greatest Greek city in the West, and only the taking of Carthage itself would have been a more difficult task. The city's defenses had long been a concern to Hiero and his predecessors, including Dionysius I, who, at the beginning of the fourth century, had concentrated on making Syracuse the most formidable military power in the Greek world. It is no surprise that Marcellus made little headway in his initial attempts to seize the city. An old man named Archimedes—who added his unique genius to the already impressive panoply of weapons, fortifications, and natural defenses that protected the city—certainly made Rome's task a more difficult one.

Traditionally, many of the weapons employed against Marcellus and the Romans at the siege of Syracuse were the work of Archimedes, the great Hellenistic Greek scientist and technological wizard. A brilliant mathematician, physicist, astronomer, engineer, mechanic, and inventor, Archimedes (c. 287–212 B.C.) was born in Syracuse. Aside from a visit to Egypt, most likely for studies at Alexandria, he appears to have remained there for the rest of his seventy-five years.

During his long career, Archimedes made numerous discoveries that would have lasting impact. Among these were his revolutionary work with gravity and leverage; his calculation of the approximate value of pi; his measurements of the sphere, the cylinder, and the cone; and the system he devised for calculating with and expressing large numbers. His pioneering work in hydrostatics produced the most enduring of the many popular stories about him. After stepping into an overfilled tub at a public bath, Archimedes suddenly realized that the water that overflowed would, if collected and measured, be equal to the volume of the body that displaced it. Since this discovery gave him the solution to a difficult problem, he supposedly got so excited that he forgot his clothes and rushed outside shouting "Eureka! Eureka!" ("I have found it!") Those observing a naked man flying past them in the street certainly must have wondered if he had not lost more than he had found!

Archimedes also constructed a celestial globe, a planetarium of sorts that [the famous later Roman orator] Cicero saw and said depicted the movement of the sun, moon, and planets and demonstrated the occurrence of eclipses. The compound pulley is thought to be his invention, as is the water screw, although it is difficult to believe that some form of water screw had not been in operation long before his day. One source says Archimedes invented it while in Egypt, where irrigation along the Nile had been going on for millennia. Perhaps he only improved upon a device he found there and brought the idea to Europe.

The accomplishments of Archimedes continued to be embellished in the centuries after his death. Fantastic devices such as a destructive heat ray were attributed to him. While the technology for the so-called burning mirrors of Archimedes was well within his grasp, and some naive modern scholars accept the ancient tradition as valid, there never was any practical application of the idea. Sources contemporary with Archimedes are silent about it, and, as one modern critic has noted, had such a device existed, it would have fallen into Roman hands when Syracuse was taken, and the Romans would gladly have employed the deadly heat ray in future wars. Even without the burning mirrors, Archimedes' engines of war were formidable. Despite his remarkable scientific and mathematical achievements, it is the legendary defense of Syracuse and his engines of destruction for which he is best remembered.

Ingenious Mechanical Devices

Ironically, Archimedes' weapons were devised when Syracuse was Rome's trusted ally. Supposedly, he himself cared little for such machines and had been persuaded by his kinsman, Hiero, the ruler of Syracuse, to provide the technical knowledge and skill to improve the city's defenses. Hiero's main concern at the time was protecting Syracuse from Carthage, not Rome. Plutarch provides a fitting, albeit colored, description of how Hiero prevailed upon Archimedes for his help. It includes a version of Archimedes' fabled assertion that provided with a big enough lever and "a place to stand . . . I will move the earth":

> . . . Archimedes had written to King Hiero, his friend and relative, that with a given force it is possible to move any given weight; and it is said that, relying on the strength of his demonstration, he even boasted that if he had another earth to stand upon he could move this one. Hiero, in amazement, begged him to put his theory into practice and to show him some great mass moved by a small force. He took a three-masted ship from the royal navy which had just been drawn out of the docks with great effort and the labor of many men; and placing in this vessel many passengers and the usual cargo, he himself sat some distance away and without any great effort, but by calmly pulling with his hand the end of the pulley, dragged the ship towards him smoothly and evenly, as if it were sailing in the sea. The king marveled at this demonstration, and having understood the power of the art, con-

vinced Archimedes to construct for him machines for all kinds of siege operations, offensive and defensive. The king never used these machines, however, since he spent most of his life in peaceful and literary pursuits. (*Marcellus* 14.7–9). . . .

Plutarch intimates that Archimedes enjoyed employing his knowledge to help protect his city. The variety, the number, and the efficiency of the weapons that were deployed along the extensive walls at Syracuse demonstrate the expense and effort Archimedes exerted in maintaining and coordinating such defenses. Hiero would not have tolerated anything less than the best. Plutarch's assertion that Archimedes was really only a dabbler and that he did not view such inventions as serious work is unrealistic:

> Archimedes possessed so elevated and profound a mind and had acquired such a wealth of scientific knowledge that although these inventions gave him a reputation of an intelligence not human, but divine, he did not want to leave behind him any writings on these matters. He considered mechanics and, in general, all the arts that touched on the needs of everyday life, as base and ignoble, and devoted his zeal only to those pure speculations whose beauty and excellence are not affected by material needs—speculations which cannot be compared to any others, and in which the proof rivals the subject, the one providing grandeur and beauty, the other accuracy and a supernatural power.

Plutarch's praise of abstract over practical knowledge does echo a real sentiment in antiquity that also had social implications. Abstract thought and theoretical discussion were associated with the wellborn, while practical application was linked, contemptuously by Aristotle and others, with those who labored manually for a living. This upper-class prejudice undoubtedly did inhibit the development of some inventions that may have benefited society, but it is an attitude that is seldom, if ever, demonstrable among the scientists and inventors themselves. The high-minded Plutarch, who knew little if anything about the real character of Archimedes, assigned him a personality so esoteric that it becomes laughable. . . .

It is clear how much the anecdotal tradition has come to cloud investigations into the real personality of Archimedes. We would probably be safe to conclude that, like Leonardo da Vinci's creations, Archimedes' mechanical devices were as much a regular part of his investigations as anything else.

The Siege of Syracuse

It is interesting that Archimedes, who had spent most of his life in a pro-Roman city led by his patron and relative, appears to have had so little difficulty turning these same weapons on his former benefactors. It may be that he never shared Hiero's high regard for Rome, or that he was first and foremost a patriot, whose primary concern was the safety of his city. Whatever his views, there is nothing to indicate that he did not devote himself wholeheartedly to the task of repelling Marcellus and his troops when they attacked in 213 B.C.

Polybius, our major source for the period, describes the greeting Archimedes had prepared for his Roman "friends" (*Histories* 8.3–7):

> . . . Archimedes had constructed the defenses of the city in such a way—both on the landward side and to repel any attack from the sea—that there was no need for the defenders to busy themselves with improvisations; instead they would have everything ready to hand, and could respond to any attack by the enemy with a counter-move. . . . [He] had constructed artillery which could cover a whole variety of ranges, so that while the attacking ships were still at a distance he scored so many hits with his catapults and stone-throwers that he was able to cause them severe damage and harass their approach. Then, as the distance decreased and these weapons began to carry over the enemy's heads, he resorted to smaller and smaller machines, and so demoralized the Romans that their advance was brought to a standstill. In the end Marcellus was reduced in despair to bringing up his ships secretly under cover of darkness. But when they had almost reached the shore, and were therefore too close to be struck by the catapults, Archimedes had devised yet another weapon to repel the marines, who were fighting from the decks. He had had the walls pierced with large numbers of

loopholes at the height of a man, which were about a palm's breadth wide at the outer surface of the walls. Behind each of these and inside the walls were stationed archers with rows of so-called "scorpions," a small catapult which discharged iron darts, and by shooting through these embrasures they put many of the marines out of action. Through these tactics he not only foiled all the enemy's attacks, both those made at long range and any attempt at hand-to-hand fighting, but also caused them heavy losses.

If any of Marcellus' ships did manage to get close enough to try to land marines, additional surprises awaited:

Against these attackers the machines could discharge stones heavy enough to drive back the marines from the bows of the ships; at the same time a grappling-iron attached to a chain would be let down, and with this the man controlling the beam would clutch at the ship. As soon as the prow was securely gripped, the lever of the machine inside the wall would be pressed down. When the operator had lifted up the ship's prow in this way and made her stand on her stern, he made fast the lower parts of the machine, so that they would not move, and finally by means of a rope and pulley suddenly slackened the grappling-iron and the chain. The result was that some of the vessels heeled over and fell on their sides, and others capsized, while the majority when their bows were let fall from a height plunged under water and filled, and thus threw all into confusion. Marcellus' operations were thus completely frustrated by these inventions of Archimedes, and when he saw that the garrison not only repulsed his attacks with heavy losses but also laughed at his efforts, he took his defeat hard. At the same time he could not refrain from making a joke against himself when he said: "Archimedes uses my ships to ladle seawater into his wine-cups. . . ."

While Marcellus had no luck attacking from the sea, Appius apparently had no better success directing the Roman land operations against Archimedes' machines and finally had to abandon his attempts:

While his troops were still at a distance from the walls they suffered many casualties from the mangonels and catapults.

This artillery was extraordinarily effective both in volume and the velocity of its fire, as was to be expected when Hiero had provided the supplies, and Archimedes designed the various engines. Then, even when the soldiers did get close to the wall, they were so harassed by the volleys of arrows and darts which continually poured through the embrasures . . . that their advance was effectually halted. Alternatively . . . they were crushed by the stones and beams that were dropped on their heads. The defenders also killed many men by means of the iron grappling hooks let down from cranes. . . . these were used to lift up men, armor and all, and then allow them to drop. In the end [Appius] withdrew to his camp and summoned a council of the military tribunes, at which it was unanimously decided to use any other methods rather than persist in the attempt to capture Syracuse by storm. And this resolution was never reversed, for during the eight months' siege of the city which followed, although they left no stratagem or daring attempt untried, they never again ventured to mount a general assault. . . . The Romans, having brought up such numerous forces both by sea and by land, had every hope of capturing the city immediately, if only one old man out of all the Syracusans could have been removed; but so long as he was present they did not dare even to attempt an attack by any method which made it possible for Archimedes to oppose them. . . .

The Fall of Syracuse

Marcellus abandoned his attempts to take the city by storm, deciding rather to blockade Syracuse and starve the population into submission. He resisted Carthaginian attempts to relieve the city, took time while Appius continued the siege to punish other anti-Roman cities in Sicily, and foiled all Syracusan attempts to break the blockade. Distracted during a festival in 212 B.C., the Syracusans became careless, and while the guards were drunk or sleeping, Marcellus led a force over the walls and captured the city's suburbs. Dogged resistance, Carthaginian interference, and a plague extended the campaign until the inner city was finally betrayed by an opportunistic Spanish mercenary who conveniently left a strategic gate unattended. Marcellus and his troops over-whelmed the remaining defenders. In late autumn of 212 B.C., Syracuse became a Roman prize, although cleanup operations did not cease until early in 211 B.C.

It was probably during the final assault on Syracuse in 212 B.C. that Archimedes perished. What actually happened to him is not known, but as might be expected, admirers contrived an end that befitted the popular concept of his life:

> Engaged in sketching a mechanical diagram, he was bending over it when a Roman came upon him and began to drag him off as a prisoner of war. Archimedes, wholly intent on his diagram and not realizing who was tugging at him, said to the man: "Away from my diagram, fellow!" Then, when the man continued to drag him along, Archimedes turned and, recognizing him for a Roman, cried out: "Quick there, one of my machines, someone!" The Roman, alarmed, slew him on the spot, a weak old man, but one whose achievements were wondrous. As soon as Marcellus learned of this, he was grieved, and together with the noblemen of the city and all the Romans gave him a splendid burial amid the tombs of his fathers. . . . (Tzetzes, *History* 2.103–149)

Other stories of his end are just as colorful—there is a strong tradition that Marcellus was greatly distressed when he learned that the great man had been killed. Not only is he supposed to have given Archimedes an appropriate burial, but he also sought out the surviving members of his family to honor them. Militarily, a living Archimedes' technological talents might have been put to good use in Rome's struggle with Hannibal (although his weapons had been designed primarily for defense), and Marcellus may have been sorry that he had missed that opportunity. Whether the Roman general's appreciation of his adversary's genius went any deeper is difficult to know. If Marcellus was so greatly upset by the loss of Archimedes, why had he not taken precautions to save him? It seems there had been opportunity to do so when representatives from Syracuse, wishing to avoid the inevitable, approached Marcellus about giving the city client-state status and placing its future in his family's hands. At that time, (or during other parleys), Marcellus could have asked that Archimedes be delivered up. Instead, he rejected all Syracusan overtures and went on to sack the city, knowing full well that any soldier could come upon Archimedes and kill him. Saving an old man who had made a fool of him and the Romans for eight months may not have been a high priority!

By exploiting the memory of the old man and his remarkable machines, Marcellus may have been trying to negate complaints in Rome about why he had taken so long to humble a stronghold of Greeks. Perhaps stories of the effectiveness of Archimedes' weapons were purposely exaggerated to mask what was, in reality, Roman incompetence. . . .

Marcellus survived Archimedes by only a few years. During his fifth consulship (208 B.C.), while carelessly reconnoitering enemy positions near the city of Venusia, the "Sword of Rome" was ambushed within sight of his camp and killed by Hannibal's troops. It was certainly an unworthy and foolish end for the man who, despite his critics, had helped guide Rome through the most difficult years of the Second Punic War.

The Romans Annihilate Carthage

Serge Lancel

The year 146 B.C. was an eventful one for Rome, which in that fateful historical moment utterly destroyed two of the greatest cities of the ancient world. One was its old archenemy Carthage, the other Corinth (in southern Greece). Ever since the end of the Second Punic War (201 B.C.), the Carthaginians had abided by the strict terms of their treaty with Rome, even in the face of constant harassment by their neighbor, and Rome's ally, the Numidian king Massinissa. But the Romans were intent on annihilating their old enemy once and for all. They therefore made completely unreasonable demands on Carthage, and when it objected, they launched the Third Punic War, summarized here by University of Grenoble scholar Serge Lancel. Under the command of Scipio Aemilianus (adoptive grandson of Scipio Africanus, who had defeated Hannibal to win the Second Punic War), a Roman army virtually eradicated Carthage. This brutal act ensured that Rome would long retain control of the of the western Mediterranean sphere. And the end of Carthage marked the conclusion of Rome's long rise to mastery of the known world.

It may be remembered that one of the clauses of the 201 treaty [ending the Second Punic War] forbade Carthage to make war—even a purely defensive one—without the agreement of the Roman people. Bound by that clause, Carthage's Senate had on several occasions during the preceding decades been forced to ask for Rome's arbitration in the dif-

Excerpted from *Carthage: A History* by Serge Lancel, translated by Antonia Nevill. Copyright © Librairie Artheme Fayard 1992. English translation, © Blackwell Publishers Ltd. 1995. Reprinted with permission.

ferences that brought it into opposition with Massinissa. In particular, a text from Polybius . . . tells us that between 165 and 162 Massinissa ravaged the region of the *Emporia*, those village ports on the Syrtis Minor, between the Gulf of Gabès and Leptis Magna, which the Carthaginians had for centuries regarded, if not as territory under their direct administration, at least in their zone of influence. Rome was alerted but remained deaf to Carthage's complaints and allowed the Numidian king to have his way. Some ten years or so later, pushing his advantage, Massinissa set about the region of the Great Plains and the Carthaginian territory known as Thusca, a vast and rich area between the middle course of the Medjerda and the wadi Siliana. Once again, the Carthaginians implored the Roman Senate, who in the end dispatched to Africa an embassy including Cato the Elder . . . but that withdrew without settling the matter. Its patience exhausted, in 151–150 the Punic State put in power representatives of the popular party, who were more inclined than the oligarchy to offer some resistance. A Punic army, commanded by Hasdrubal the Boetharch ('commander of the auxiliary troops'), came to confront the Numidians in the defence of a town called Oroscopa, the location of which remains unknown. After an initial engagement with no decisive outcome, Hasdrubal's troops, surrounded and brought down by starvation, had to yield and were treacherously massacred. Massinissa thus stayed as master of his new conquests, which brought him to the very gates of Carthage's land.

But worst of all, Rome decided to use the opportunity of that desperate attempt to put an end to matters with its old enemy. Did the latest of Massinissa's successes arouse Rome's fear that he was on the point of achieving his ultimate aim . . . of creating on Carthage's ruins a native kingdom the size of almost the entire present-day Maghreb, which would make him a force to be reckoned with? There are some historians who see the cause of the third Punic War in that concern. But it has also been pointed out that in 150 the Numidian prince, then aged eighty-eight years and on the point of disappearing, could hardly count on his heirs— in a succession that promised to be as difficult as the one which had brought him to power himself over half a century before—to realize such a grandiose enterprise. . . .

The Romans' Brutal, Inhumane Demand

Rome opted for war, but did not declare it and concealed its intentions. However, at Carthage it was known that mobilization was taking place in Italy. Fear triumphed over the pride that had inspired resistance to the Numidian prince. Utica, scenting a change in the wind, defected and placed itself under the protection of Rome. Hasdrubal, condemned to death as the scapegoat, managed to escape, but the oligarchy, led by Hanno, returned to power and decided to trust in the 'good faith' of the Romans, sending an embassy to Rome which arrived there at the beginning of 149.

Meanwhile, on the Roman side, all arrangements had been made for war. The two consuls, Manilius and Censorinus, had already concentrated in Sicily the expeditionary corps and the fleet that would soon transport it to Africa. In Rome, the Punic embassy that had just made an act of submission before the Senate was given to understand that Carthage, as a pledge of its loyalty, must deliver 300 hostages within thirty days to the consuls at their headquarters in Sicily.

It was at Utica, where in the spring of 149 the consuls had just installed themselves and their troops, that the Punic delegation finally learned Rome's wishes: Carthage was to hand over all its weapons and war machines. Despite the protests of the people, the Carthaginian Senate complied. . . . That done, it only remained to unveil to the disarmed Carthaginians the final phase of a plan that had been carefully kept secret. It was imparted at Utica to a deputation made up of thirty of the Punic state's principal men: the Carthaginians could remain free to live according to their laws, on condition that they abandoned their city, which Rome had determined to destroy, to go and settle wherever they pleased, provided it was at least eighty stadia (about fifteen kilometres) from the sea.

Such a diktat [demand] was the equivalent of a death sentence. There was no precedent in Antiquity for a state's surviving the eradication of what constituted it on the sacred plane: the destruction of its temples and cemeteries, the deportation of its cults, were a more surely mortal blow than displacing the population. But that displacement in itself, simply in material and non-religious terms, was the very negation of what for centuries had been the vocation and *raison d'être* [reason for being] of Carthage, a maritime State whose power and wealth relied on the feelers it sent out from its ports across the seas. . . .

If the Roman consuls had hoped to spare themselves a war by persuading the Carthaginians to perform collective suicide, they were disappointed. When Rome's diktat was announced, popular fury swiftly followed despondency. As well as the representatives bringing the terrible tidings, senators accused of treason and Italian traders who happened to be in Carthage fell victim to it and were massacred. There was a rush to the city gates to close them, while the Carthaginian Senate decreed a state of war and freed slaves in order to enrol them. The 'boetharch' named Hasdrubal, who ran the campaign with about 20,000 men, was entreated to forget the death sentence against him and to direct military operations outside the town, while a general bearing the same name was charged with the defence of the town. . . . Energy born of despair performed prodigious feats: each day, improvised arsenals manufactured 100 shields, 300 swords, 500 javelins, 1000 projectiles for the catapults. The women of Carthage offered their gold and, so it is said, gave their hair to be used as ropes for the machines.

Initial Roman Offensives

The two Roman consuls without doubt underestimated that heroic determination. At all events, they were in no hurry to lay siege to a town that was still inadequately defended. . . . It was not until the summer of 149 that the place was finally attacked, Manilius' mission being to break through its fortifications on the side of the isthmus, while Censorinus gave himself the task of attacking the theoretically weaker part of the great enclosing wall, the one which, to the south, linked the defences of the isthmus with the entry to the ports, running along the north shore of Lake Tunis.

It did not take the Roman generals long to realize that seizing Carthage by sheer force, even when it had been disarmed by treachery, would be an arduous undertaking. In the manner of many large towns in the Hellenistic era, the town properly speaking, but also its *suburbia*, its residential quarters and surrounding semi-rural suburbs, were enclosed within a vast fortified envelope which protected the whole of the peninsula. . . .

It was this . . . defence that the consul Manilius attacked during the summer of 149. His first attempt was in vain. But the account of it that has come down to us throws some light on the nature of the fortification: Manilius had first to fill in the trench (*taphros*), then force the small wall (*brachu epiteichisma*), that is, the parapet surmounting it, before setting about the high walls (*upsèla teichè*). The Roman consul tried again shortly afterwards but . . . he finally had to give up attacking on that side, after a great amount of effort that resulted only in making a breach in the outer wall. . . .

At its southern extremity this . . . fortification made an angle, from which was born the single wall going alongside Lake Tunis to join the harbour area, south of the town. During the summer of 149 it was the lot of Censorinus, the second consul, in command of the fleet, to attack this wall, concentrating . . . on its 'single corner', with the help of ladders set up on the lake shore, or from vessels moored on the lake near to its bank. This attempt having failed twice, Censorinus set up his camp at the foot of the rampart, on the lake shore. A little later . . . the consul partially filled in the lake to give himself more room to manoeuvre his siege machines, in particular his two battering-rams, one of which, manned by 6000 soldiers, succeeded in breaking down part of the wall, thus allowing the Romans to penetrate through the breach but without managing to maintain their hold there. . . . As the scorching midsummer heat had arrived—thus at the height of summer 149—he [Censorinus] could not stay long at the foot of that wall whose height prevented him from taking advantage of the off-sea breeze, those refreshing winds which, during Carthage's summer, come from the north-north-east quarter. It was for this reason that the consul then moved his camp seawards, setting it up on the sandy strip . . . near the mouth of the harbours that would become the bridgehead from which the final assault would be launched in 147.

Meanwhile 149 came to an end without the Romans being able to take advantage of the difficult position of Carthage. . . .

At the beginning of 148, sensing that his end was nigh, Massinissa sent for Scipio Aemilianus to come to his capital, to help him settle the succession of the Numidian kingdom he had received from Africanus. But by the time Scipio Aemilianus arrived at Cirta (Constantine) the old king had died. Having the authority to arbitrate, the Roman officer arranged the succession judiciously . . . dividing the royal power among the three legitimate sons. . . . Shortly afterwards, he obtained another success with the surrender of Hasdrubal's chief lieutenant, Phamaias, who went over to the Roman camp with more than 2000 of his men. The rest of 148 passed with the position unaltered in Carthage. The two consuls leaving office were succeeded by L. Calpurnius Piso, who chose as legate L. Hostilius Mancinus, entrusted with the fleet. The two new leaders opted to carry on the war against those cities which had remained loyal to the Punic capital, to bring them down and thus deprive the Carthaginians of resources of food and manpower. . . .

Scipio Aemilianus Takes Command

In the spring of 147 Mancinus, cruising with the fleet off the coast of Carthage, noticed that in the north sector of the town, on the Megara side, the rampart was poorly defended where the rocky coast made access difficult, either in the vicinity of Gammarth, or more probably where the heights of Sidi-bou-Saïd plunge into the sea by way of cliffs or steep slopes. A detachment of a few dozen men was sent to scale those slopes and prepare to get over the wall. The Carthaginians, seeing them raising their ladders, came out through a postern but were put to flight by the men in the commando group, who were then joined by Mancinus and the main body of the troop and gained a foothold inside the wall. But that improvised attack, carried out by men who were inadequately armed and without victuals, was in danger of turning into a disaster. The next day Mancinus and his men, numbering several hundred, had been driven back against the wall by the Carthaginians and were about to be crushed when they were saved by the unexpected intervention of Scipio Aemilianus.

Although he was not yet of the required age to fill this office . . . the people made sure that he was appointed by name to command the army in Africa, instead of lots being drawn between the two consuls of the year. Scipio Aemilianus made up the necessary numbers by enlistment and landed at Utica, taking with him as lieutenant his most faithful friend, C. Laelius, and accompanied by two of the foremost Greeks, the philosopher Panaetius of Rhodes and the historian Polybius. His arrival at Utica happened to coincide with Mancinus' improvised expedition, and he at once went to his rescue. . . .

In this war of positions, shutting all Carthage's defenders within its walls was a turning-point that proved decisive. Scipio finished sealing them in by cutting off the isthmus, parallel with the Punic fortification, with an entrenched camp of a rectangular layout provided with towers, the middle one of which, topped by a high watchtower, allowed observation of everything that was happening in the Punic camp. Shortly afterwards, to complete the blockade and render any reprovisioning by sea virtually impossible, the Roman general decided to close access to the ports by constructing a mole in the direction of their pierhead; its exact line is still disputed, as no trace of it has been discovered. . . .

A bitter struggle then began in this sector of the harbours. The Carthaginians had not waited until work on the mole was completed before finding an answer. Secretly, working mainly at night to avoid being seen, they prepared a new access to their harbours on the east side, probably starting from the circular basin of the military harbour, and at the same time contrived to fit out a small combat fleet with used materials and old patched-up boats. When both the ships and the new channel were ready, they made a breach in the wall of the town's sea front. Through that exit went several dozen triremes and quinqueremes, and a quantity of other smaller boats. The effect was one of total surprise, and the only mistake the Carthaginians made . . . was not to take more advantage of it.

A mole is a dam, but it is also a bridge thrown from one point to another, and Scipio intended to use it in this way, to gain a foothold on the shelf of the outer harbour. . . . On this quay the besieged had constructed an additional rampart, the better to defend it. Scipio had his siege machines moved along the roadway of the mole, and the Carthaginians burned them the first time in a desperate sortie. However, the attacker had the last word, establishing himself firmly on the landing stage and, in his turn, building a fortification to counter the low Punic rampart, from which the defenders were finally driven. At the beginning of the winter of 147–146, 4000 men were posted there by Scipio to hold this highly strategic point. . . .

The Final Assault

One day in March or April 146 the final assault was ordered. It started from the quay of the outer harbour that had been held and fortified for several months by Scipio's men. Hasdrubal, believing that the attack would first target the rectangular basin of the merchant harbour, which in fact lay next to the quay, set fire to the neighbouring buildings, no doubt wooden warehouses. But Laelius, commanding the manoeuvre at that moment, made for the circular port and got his soldiers across its double enclosure by means of improvised bridges. The besieged were at the end of their strength and offered little resistance. Near the war harbour—and thus slightly north of this basin—stretched the esplanade of the great public square, the *agora*, of Greek texts. Scipio took possession of it and, as night had fallen, advanced no farther and camped there with his men. Next morning, the soldiers rewarded themselves for their trouble by invading the temple of Apollo, which apparently gave on to the square, and detaching with their sword-points the gold plates adorning the tabernacle of the god's chapel, in order to share them out.

The defences of the lower town having yielded, the final

objective was the citadel of Byrsa, the last bastion of resistance, where tens of thousands of men, women and children had taken refuge. The consul called on 4000 men who had not yet been in the fight and made them converge on the citadel, in particular, making them advance along three streets which ascended to it from the square. These streets . . . were bordered by six-storeyed houses, from the tops of which the Roman soldiers were attacked with all kinds of projectiles. . . . That advance was difficult. They had to gain mastery over each of these houses in turn, and on reaching their roofs pass from one to the other, getting over the street space by means of beams used as makeshift bridges; the width of the cross streets in the quarter unearthed on Byrsa—averaging five metres—does not rule out the possibility of such a feat.

Meanwhile fighting was raging in the streets, where bodies hurled down from the upper floors added to the victims of the mêlée at ground level. [The Greek historian] Appian has described these nightmare scenes with a precision of horrific detail unprecedented in an ancient account of this kind. A notable example is when the area had been delivered to the flames block by block and the walls knocked down, and the street cleaners came in the wake of the soldiers, with the task of clearing space for the passage of further attacking waves. . . . Army servants used hooks to drag both dead and living to be flung pell-mell, with the debris of the houses, into pits from which still-moving heads and limbs could sometimes be seen emerging, only to be crushed by the galloping horses. Those atrocious scenes were the savage harvest of so much hatred sown on both sides. . . .

Six days and nights passed in this way. On the seventh, some of the besieged emerged from the citadel and came to implore Scipio to spare the lives of at least those who surrendered. And out came some 50,000 survivors to whom Scipio granted their lives, and who ended their days in slavery. There remained nearly a thousand renegades, who could expect no mercy; they sought a last refuge in the temple of Eschmoun, where they were joined by Hasdrubal and his family. At the last moment the Punic general weakened;

holding a suppliant's branch, he came to prostrate himself before Scipio, begging for pity. The cowardice of a man was redeemed by a woman: dressed as if for a festival, Hasdrubal's wife stood on the high wall of the temple, facing the Roman general and her husband, whom she reproached for his betrayal. Then she cast herself and her children into the flames of the temple, which the renegades had set ablaze, and there they perished. . . .

Endless Night Falls on Carthage

Throughout its history Carthage had always glowed red with the light of pyres. The one that consumed the city—and archaeologists find the carbonized layer everywhere, compacted by the centuries—lasted another ten days. In 212 Marcellus had wept over the beauty of Syracuse, which his soldiers were making ready to take by storm and devastate. In front of the fire that destroyed Carthage Scipio, it is said, shed tears and spoke aloud these lines from Homer: 'A day will come when Ilium [Troy], that holy town, will perish, and Priam also will perish, and his people, so skilled in handling the spear' (*Iliad*, IV, 164–5). And in answer to Polybius, who asked him the reason for the quotation, he is said to have replied that he feared lest it might one day be used in regard to his own homeland. . . . The cries ringing in his ears as Carthage burned were the cries of the town martyred above all others, the cries that ceaselessly obsessed Antiquity, . . . cries whose echo has not completely faded, those of the 'cruel night which for an entire people was an eternal night', as [the seventeenth-century French playwright] Racine would say.

Carthage entered its own night, and silence fell on the ruins of what had been one of the most beautiful towns in the ancient world.

Chapter 4

Conquest of the Greeks

Turning Points

IN WORLD HISTORY

The Roman and Greek Military Systems Compared

Archer Jones

Archer Jones, a noted military historian who has taught at several universities, here compares the two major, competing military systems—the Greek and Roman—that existed in the third century B.C., when Rome first began to oppose the Greek states. He begins with a brief overview of the combined, or integrated, military system developed in the fourth century B.C. by King Philip II and his son Alexander the Great, both of the Greek kingdom of Macedonia. Their system, like other Greek ones before it, was based mainly on the formidable, but ultimately monolithic and inflexible phalanx battle formation. Jones then describes the Roman system, perfected little by little in costly encounters with various enemies, notably the Greek general Pyrrhus and Carthaginian general Hannibal (who was eventually defeated by Rome's Scipio Africanus). The Roman system was based on battalions called legions, which on the battlefield broke down into smaller, more flexible units—the maniples. Finally, Jones cites some of Rome's first battles fought on Greek soil to show how the Roman system proved more flexible and effective. (The terms "heavy" and "light" in reference to infantry and cavalry generally differentiate heavily armored fighters from those wearing little or no armor. The quotes that appear throughout the essay are by the second-century-B.C. Greek historian Polybius.)

Philip bequeathed to Alexander a force of heavy cavalry. Whereas Greek and Persian cavalry used the javelin or the

Excerpted from *The Art of War in the Western World* by Archer Jones (New York: Oxford University Press). Copyright © 1987 by the Board of Trustees of the University of Illinois. Reprinted by permission of the University of Illinois Press.

bow and were prepared to thrust with a javelin or light spear, some Macedonian cavalry relied primarily on shock action [frontal assaults on enemy infantry and cavalry]. Like the heavy infantry, these men wore armor and carried shields and a short lance, a cavalry spear. About nine feet long and weighing four pounds, the lance had an iron point on each end. Though the horseman lacked a stirrup, training and practice enabled him to keep his seat reasonably well in combat at close quarters. When he thrust with his lance, he released it at or just before the moment of impact to avoid transmitting to himself the shock of the blow. He thus escaped the danger of losing his seat on his mount.

The Macedonian Combined Weapons System

Macedonian horsemen also differed from Greek cavalry in that they were thoroughly disciplined and trained to work together in groups and to respond to commands. They thus had better articulation, training, and skill in addition to their primary reliance on shock action. Over cavalry relying on javelins and rarely closing with the enemy, this doctrine enabled them to enjoy the same advantage as Greek heavy infantry held over light infantry in shock combat. Cavalry unprepared for determined shock action could not resist their charge. Heavy cavalry had the same dominance over light infantry as did heavy infantry, with an important difference—light infantry could not escape by running away. Only the heavy infantry, a formation of armored hoplites with their spears, could resist the charge and best them in hand-to-hand combat.

This Macedonian heavy cavalry, a small elite group, was called Companions of the King. The Macedonian army also had far more of the traditional, hybrid, or general-purpose cavalry, which largely relied on missile action, principally the javelin. And the bulk of the Macedonian army remained infantry. Light infantry had an important role: in battle it deployed in front of the heavy infantry where it could use its traditional tactics of slinging missiles, shooting arrows, or hurling javelins while keeping away from its heavy infantry opponents. Before the lines of hoplites clashed, the light infantry withdrew out of harm's way, its usefulness ended. Thus the tactics involved an initial reliance on the intrinsic ascendancy of the light over the heavy infantry.

The Macedonians changed the heavy infantry by doubling the length of the spear, at least for the ranks behind the first two. The longer spear enabled those of several ranks to project beyond the front, utilizing more rear-rank men and making an advance by this phalanx formidable indeed. Even if the front ranks did not use shorter spears and the rear ranks progressively longer spears, a united push by several ranks almost always drove back the opponents. The longer spears also made body armor less important, the rear ranks requiring none at all, a substantial saving in equipment costs. Relying more on the action of the group, individual soldiers needed less skill. Still the Macedonians made a virtue of the tactical innovation of the long spear and drilled their phalanx of professional soldiers so that it could function as a unit. In addition, they subdivided their troops, giving some articulation and maneuverability to an inherently unwieldy formation. But the longer spear reflected a subtle change, placing greater reliance on the advance of a wall of spears and less on the individual effort by the men in the front rank.

The creators of this army, the astute Philip and his son, Alexander, integrated these four weapon systems into a mutually supporting combat team. Heavy and light infantry each had its role as did the light and heavy cavalry, with the shock action of the elite Companions of the King held for a decisive blow. No weapon system had primacy, and none a merely auxiliary role; all had a significant part to play. . . .

Roman Weapons and Battlefield Units

While the Macedonians were perfecting the art of war in their fashion, the army of Rome, a small Italian city-state, evolved in a different direction. Like the Greeks, the Romans fought with a phalanx of hoplites assisted by light infantry and a general-purpose cavalry. But the Romans abandoned the spear as their principal weapon fairly early and adopted versatile offensive arms. For defense, they placed heavy reliance on a large convex shield, two and a half feet wide and four feet high. This wooden shield, covered with cloth and then with calf skin and reinforced in the center with iron, could turn "aside the more formidable blows of stones, pikes, and heavy missiles in general." A contemporary explained that "its upper and lower rims are strengthened by an iron edging which protects it from descending blows and from injury when resting on the ground." Since the Romans engaged in many sieges, faced the long pikes or spears of the Greeks, and fought the Celts who wielded a two-handed cutting sword, they eventually devised a shield effective against all opponents. They completed their protection with a helmet and a brass breastplate or, for the wealthier, a coat of chain-mail.

For attack the Romans depended for shock combat on a short sword, "excellent for thrusting, and both of its edges cut effectually, as the blade is very strong and firm." Such a sword would prove its worth at close quarters with an opponent whose two-handed sword or long pike could be turned aside by the shield. The bulk of the infantry also carried two of a javelin called a pilum. This had a point that bent or broke if it struck a hard object so that "the enemy is unable to return it. If this were not so, the missile would be available to both sides." This suited Roman tactics, which consisted of throwing the javelin and then closing quickly to fight with sword and shield.

The distinctive organization matured by the Romans proved more fundamental than their use of the sword. Arraying their army in three successive lines, each six ranks deep, they subdivided these lines into maniples, each maniple having two centuries of sixty men each. This subdivision provided rudimentary articulation and promised some maneuverability. The Romans exploited this organization by leaving gaps between each maniple in each line; the maniples of the second line were staggered so that they covered the gaps in the first. The third line differed from the first two as its maniples had only half the front, with sixty rather than 120 men. The men of the third line were the older citizens and still used the spear as their principal weapon. The maniples of the third line positioned themselves behind the holes in the second line, making the whole formation somewhat like a checkerboard. This was the basic formation in which the Romans advanced to the fight. Since gaps would almost certainly form in any line of battle as it advanced, the Romans anticipated this by providing the intervals systematically. Before the Roman line closed with the enemy in combat, the second line filled the breaks in the first with either a century or a full maniple pushing into the spaces in the front line. The third line moved up into the vacant positions in the second line and, with the remainder of the second line, constituted a reserve if not needed to help fill a large gap in the first line. This organization gave the Roman line of battle a flexibility and responsiveness that the phalanx lacked.

The administrative organization provided another element of strength in the Roman system. Ten of the first- and second-line maniples of 120 men each and ten of the sixty-man third-line maniples comprised an administrative organization called a legion. With a proportion of orderlies, clerks, porters, etc., some of whom doubled as light infantry, and a small amount of cavalry, the legion numbered over 4,000 men. When the Romans expanded their army, they added legions, thus providing good administration and organization for any large field army. . . .

The Romans practiced a slow but sure strategy, and gradually Rome dominated much of Italy. Since political astuteness complemented military skill, they bound to themselves as firm and willing allies the areas they controlled and extended to these allies the Roman organization and style of warfare. By the time of Alexander the Great, Rome had become a formidable power, ready to come into military contact with others in the Mediterranean.

Rome's First Encounters with the Macedonian System

The Macedonian system as used by Alexander became the standard for the eastern Mediterranean and much of the old Persian Empire. The difference between the Macedonian and Roman systems lay not primarily in the Roman use of swords and the Macedonian reliance on the spear; the difference was more subtle. The Roman army depended on their sword-wielding, partially articulated heavy infantry with their light infantry and cavalry filling the roles of auxiliaries. In their evolution from the phalanx to the manipular array, they had improved the infantry but had not developed in the direction of the Macedonian system of Alexander, which relied on the combined effect of all arms, including a cavalry force trained for real shock combat.

In the first major Roman combat with the Macedonian or Alexandrian system the combined-arms force won. The particulars of these battles with King Pyrrhus of the Greek Kingdom of Epirus are obscure, but, in Pyrrhus, the Romans faced not only a relative and disciple of Alexander the Great but also a general whose many campaigns had earned for him a most exalted reputation. The Romans attributed much of Pyrrhus's success to his use of elephants, which Alexander's successors had incorporated into the Macedonian system after Alexander faced them in India. Often unreliable, occasionally stampeding through their own infantry when attacked by javelins and other missiles, elephants proved most effective against cavalry because they frightened the enemy's horses. Pyrrhus based his successful battles with the Romans not on his elephants but on the success of his cavalry, presumably aided by elephants, in defeating the Roman cavalry and attacking the Roman infantry in flank and rear. But in defeat the Romans inflicted such severe ca-

Hannibal rides an elephant in a victory parade, perhaps after defeating the Romans at the Trebia River in 218 B.C.

sualties on Pyrrhus that he remarked that more such victories would force him to return to Greece alone.

In its first contest with the Romans, the African power Carthage copied the Macedonian system of war, even retaining a Greek general to command the army in the campaign to drive back the Roman invasion of Africa. Stationed as usual, on the flanks, the more powerful heavy cavalry of the Carthaginians defeated the Roman cavalry on the flanks and attacked the Roman infantry in the rear. The articulation inherent in the Roman three-line system meant that the rear maniples could turn about to fend off this assault, but this effective defensive tactic did not save the Romans: the Carthaginians won the Battle of Tunis and captured the Roman commander. . . .

The Roman System Proves Itself at Zama

[After more defeats, including the loss of some 50,000 men at Cannae, in 216 B.C.] the Romans avoided battle with Hannibal for fourteen years. When they again met him, they had in their commander, Scipio, a brilliant general who, though in his early thirties, had ample experience. . . . In spite of his taste for luxury and his Greek culture, Scipio easily instilled confidence in his troops. He then led his army into Africa while the steadfast Hannibal still remained in southern Italy. By this time the Romans no longer fielded militia, and Scipio commanded and inspired the devotion of an army largely composed of well-trained and disciplined veterans of many campaigns. Scipio and Hannibal met in Africa in 202 B.C. at the Battle of Zama, where each exhibited his genius. The contest between these two masters advanced the art of war. . . .

The Roman army had decisive superiority in cavalry, an advantage that usually belonged to Hannibal. But Scipio did not rely exclusively on his cavalry for success. He deployed his infantry in a manner that he had developed in Spain. Instead of having the maniples of the second and third lines close to and covering the intervals in the first line, he kept them back a distance of probably several hundred feet. He correctly believed that when the six-deep first line engaged the enemy infantry, the veterans would manage well without additional ranks behind them. The rear ranks constituted Scipio's reserve. . . .

But Scipio also had to cope with the Carthaginian army's eighty elephants. For this reason he abandoned the usual Roman initial array in a checkerboard formation and stationed the second and third lines of maniples directly behind those of the first. The intervals of the first he filled with the light infantry, "ordering them to open the action, and if they were forced back by the charge of the elephants to retire, those who had time to do so by the straight passages as far to the rear of the whole army, and those who were overtaken to right or left along the intervals between the lines."

Hannibal, realizing that he could not rely on his cavalry for victory, also had in a rear line of infantry a reserve that he could deploy. As at Cannae his best troops made up this reserve, but he altered his disposition of them. At Cannae he had placed the reserve in a column on each flank of his infantry line, ready to advance, face, and attack the Romans in their flank. But, since such a disposition was too obvious against Scipio, he kept this reserve in line, behind and parallel to his main infantry line. Superior in infantry, Hannibal counted on winning by using his reserve to envelop the Roman infantry line.

When the battle opened and as the light cavalry skirmished between the lines, "Hannibal ordered the drivers of the elephants to charge the enemy. When the trumpets and bugles sounded shrilly from all sides, some of the animals took fright and at once turned tail and rushed back" upon the Carthaginians. But some of the unpredictable and dangerous beasts did go forward against the Roman line, faced the javelins of the courageous Roman light infantry, "and finally in their terror escaped through the gaps in the Roman line which Scipio's foresight had provided." Others fled to the flanks, clearing the field for the serious engagement of the infantry and cavalry.

Then the imposing lines of the Roman and Carthaginian heavy infantry joined battle. Meanwhile, the Roman . . . cavalry had driven Hannibal's cavalry from the field and, as Hannibal doubtless had anticipated, instead of attacking the Carthaginian infantry, had pursued the fleeing enemy cavalry far from the field of battle. This often happened in battle, commanders being unable to control their cavalrymen who naturally sought to follow their beaten foes. At Cannae Hannibal's well-disciplined and well-led professional cavalry had immediately turned against the rear of the Roman infantry, but at Zama the Roman and allied cavalry lacked the discipline, restraint, and leadership to enable them to make this critical maneuver.

With all cavalry off the field of battle, Hannibal had an infantry battle alone and moved promptly to exploit his numerical superiority and the articulation provided by his reserve of veterans. He moved out his rear infantry formation, extending its line preparatory to enveloping the flanks of the Roman infantry. But Scipio saw the maneuver in time to commit his rear-line reserve, extending his line equally, and the infantry of the two armies remained locked in a frontal battle of doubtful outcome. Then, before the infantry battle reached a decision, the Roman . . . cavalry returned to the battlefield and carried out their mission of attacking the rear of the relatively thin, fully committed line of Carthaginian infantry. This decided the battle, the Romans . . . virtually annihilating the Carthaginian army, leaving a field covered with "slippery corpses which were still soaked in blood and had fallen in heaps."

The role of the cavalry in the Roman victory at Zama revealed that the Romans had adopted the Macedonian system. But the use of a reserve by both combatants and the superior articulation that made this possible shows that the art of war had surpassed that of Alexander's era. Neither Hannibal nor Scipio had participated in the battle, both remaining where they could manage the contest and commit their reserves at the critical time and place. This represented a major advance over Alexander's preplanned battles, as did the concept of the subtracted or uncommitted reserve and the improved articulation of the infantry that enabled the reserves to maneuver on the battlefield. The excellent articulation of the Roman army had done much to permit Scipio to command all of the army in battle rather than, as had Alexander, only a part. . . .

Roman Legions Against the Hellenistic Phalanx

When the Romans fought in Greece and Asia, they again confronted the Macedonian system of war. Although the Romans also used this combined-arms method, they still stressed their heavy infantry and never raised their cavalry to the quality or the importance that it had with Alexander. But they also never had to make war with the united forces of Alexander's by-then divided empire, and they almost always fought with the aid of local allies. The Romans had critical help from an ally in their major battle against their most-imposing opponent, Antiochus the Great, ruler of Syria and much of Asia to the east. In the conflict in 190 B.C. at Magnesia in Asia Minor, they faced a formidable army under Antiochus himself with the exiled Hannibal as his advisor. The details of the battle are vague, but clearly the powerful cavalry of the Roman ally, the king of Pergamum, played an important role in the Roman victory. Increasingly the Romans relied on their allies to provide cavalry.

The apparent challenge to the dominance of the Romans' tactical system came not from the possibility that their opponents might have superior cavalry but from a further development of the Macedonian phalanx. When in 197 B.C. the Romans faced an army of the Macedonian kingdom, they found that the phalanx had lengthened at least some of its spears to twenty-one feet. Apparently the front ranks had shorter spears, probably nine feet, which they held in one hand; the fifth rank used both hands to carry twenty-one-foot spears that projected beyond the front rank; the intermediate ranks seem to have had spears of varying lengths so that all the spear points projected about the same distance beyond the front rank. The front ranks carried shields; the rear rank, using both hands to hold their long spear, had either no shields or very small ones slung on a strap across their chests. Behind the first five ranks the phalanx had an additional eleven ranks, the men holding their spears elevated until needed.

This formation marched shoulder-to-shoulder and for its effectiveness relied on the combined effect of the spears; the individual had no role except to hold his spear and keep his formation. Since the Romans fought with swords and so

needed more space between them than the men in the phalanx, the phalanx had two men in front for every Roman. Each
Roman thus faced ten spears. According to the historian Polybius, "It is both impossible for a single man to cut through
them all in time once they are at close quarters and by no
means easy to force their points away." It seemed, therefore,
that this new phalanx could bear down all opposition, giving
the Macedonians victory because of their better infantry.

But the articulated Roman infantry easily defeated this apparently invincible tactical innovation. In connection with
their success at the Battle of Zama, Polybius had pointed out
that the subdivided Roman tactical organization enabled
"every man individually and in common with his fellows to
present a front in any direction, the maniples which are nearest to the danger turning themselves by a single movement to
face it. Their arms also give the men both protection and confidence owing to the size of the shield and owing to the sword
being strong enough to endure repeated blows." Thus the
Roman could maneuver, and if he could get past the hoplite's
spear, he had overwhelming superiority at close quarters, especially against the shieldless men with the two-handed spears.

In the first conflict the Romans won the infantry combat
because they caught the phalanx before it had formed and
while some of its members were still marching to the place of
battle. But even under favorable conditions the phalanx depended so much upon keeping its formation that it could
never have succeeded against the Roman infantry. Polybius
pointed out, "The phalanx requires level and clear ground
with no obstacles such as ditches, clefts, clumps of trees, ridges
and water courses, all of which are sufficient to impede and
break up such a formation." Of course, gaps in a phalanx
would enable the Roman swordsmen to come to close quarters
with disastrous consequence for the hoplites in the phalanx.

Even on level ground the phalanx proved vulnerable, for,
Polybius wrote, "the Romans do not make their line equal in
force to the enemy and expose all of the legions to a frontal attack by the phalanx, but part of their forces remain in reserve
and the rest engaged the enemy. Afterwards whether the phalanx drives back by its charge the force opposed to it or is re-

pulsed by this force," the phalanx exposes itself either "in following up a retreating foe or in flying before an attacking foe." When this happens, the phalanx then leaves "behind the other parts of their own army, upon which" the Roman "reserve have room enough in the space formerly held by the phalanx to attack no longer in front" but appear "by a lateral movement on the flank and rear of the phalanx" and so with sword and shield at close quarters on the flank slaughter the hoplites whose formation and weapons made them almost defenseless.

Thus the improved infantry of the Romans helped Rome establish its mastery over the Mediterranean basin. The Romans had incorporated all of the features of the Macedonian system and had learned from Hannibal the value of an infantry reserve and the concept of a general who kept out of combat so that he could control the reserve and direct the battle.

Rome's Subjugation of the Greeks Begins

Arthur E.R. Boak and William G. Sinnigen

Besides the defeat and eradication of Carthage, the other major development concluding Rome's rise to mastery over most of the known world was the subjugation of the Greek states clustered in the eastern Mediterranean. (These included the Macedonian Kingdom, encompassing most of northern Greece; the Seleucid Kingdom, occupying large parts of nearby Asia Minor and the Near East; the Aetolian Confederacy, an alliance of cities in central Greece that had banded together for mutual protection; and a number of individual mainland and island city-states.) This large-scale clash between the Romans and Greeks was perhaps inevitable. But the Romans needed an excuse for initiating it and one of the leading Greek rulers of the day conveniently provided it. Philip V, king of the Macedonian Kingdom, made the mistake of allying himself with Carthage during the Second Punic War. On the pretext of punishing Philip for this affront, late in 200 B.C. the Romans crossed the Adriatic Sea into Illyria, the Balkan region bordering Macedonia in the west. Soon afterward they entered Greece, and within only a few years managed to defeat not only Philip, but also the able and energetic Seleucid ruler Antiochus III and the feisty Aetolians. The following summary of these initial Roman interventions in Greek affairs is by former University of Michigan professor Arthur E.R. Boak and former Hunter College professor William G. Sinnigen.

During the thirty-five years which followed the battle of Zama, Rome attained the same dominant position in the eastern Mediterranean that she had won in the West as a result of the First and Second Punic Wars. The explanation of Roman interference in the East and the rapid extension of her authority there lies in the political situation of the Hellenistic world at the close of the third century, one which Rome exploited by virtue of her increasingly important role as patron to states east of the Adriatic. . . .

Down to the year 201 Rome can hardly be said to have had any definite eastern policy. Diplomatic intercourse with Egypt had followed the visit of an Egyptian embassy to Rome as early as 273, but this had had no political consequences. Since that date she had come into conflict with the Illyrians and with Macedonia and had established a small protectorate across the Adriatic, but in so doing her actions had been spasmodic and had been brought about by the attacks of the Illyrians and Macedonians upon her allies or herself and were not the result of any aggressive policy of her own. The interest and outlook of Rome's agrarian oligarchy did not include Hellas [Greece] as a whole or the Greek East. This may be seen in the favorable peace terms granted Philip V of Macedonia in 205, by which Rome abandoned her formal alliances with Philip's enemies, especially the Aetolians. This is the first known instance in which Rome failed to fulfill to the letter her written agreements with her friends, and marks an important stage in the growing sophistication of her foreign policy. These actions made her very unpopular in most of Greece. Her erstwhile allies, especially the Aetolians, protested that they had been left in the lurch, while other Greek states felt antagonistic because Rome had permitted the Aetolians to treat them brutally during the recent war. Rome still found it possible to maintain friendly relations, albeit without formal and possibly entangling treaties, with Pergamon, the Illyrians, some city-states of the Peloponnesus, and possibly Athens. Rome's general attitude toward the Greek world in the period 205–201 was watchful rather than disinterested; she had no vital or definite commitments in the area except the defense of her Illyrian clients.

The Romans Turn Eastward

A combination of circumstances involving Illyria brought about the Second Macedonian War. After the peace of 205 Philip apparently misread the Roman attitude toward Greece as one of total disinterest and attempted by diplomacy to seduce the Illyrians from their connection with Rome. Just as Rome was observing the Illyrian situation with increasing disquiet in 202, the envoys of Rhodes and of Attalus I, King of Pergamon, arrived to inform the Senate of Philip's aggressions in the East and of his alleged pact with Antiochus to partition the Egyptian Empire. They requested Roman help. The Senate, basically unconcerned with what was going on in the Aegean and undisturbed by the unlikely prospect of the "alliance" between Philip and Antiochus being directed against Italy at some future date, was interested, however, in humbling the king who had stabbed her in the back during the recent war with Hannibal and who was now tampering with her Illyrian clients. It seized upon Philip's aggressions against Attalus as possible *casus belli* [justification for war]. Roman ambassadors were sent to Greece in 201/200 to proclaim a basic change in Roman policy—protection of all Greeks against future Macedonian aggression—and to mobilize Greece under the Roman aegis against Philip. They also carried an ultimatum for Philip which they delivered to one of his generals, a demand that he refrain from war with any Greek state and that he submit his differences with Attalus to arbitration. The ultimatum revealed Rome's new aims: the reduction of Philip to the status of a client prince and the consequent conversion of Greece into a Roman protectorate. Although the Senate was apparently committed to war when these demands were not met, the Roman people as a whole shrank from embarking upon another war so soon after the close of the desperate conflict with Carthage. At first the Centuriate Assembly voted against the proposal, and at a second meeting was induced to sanction it only when the people were told they would have to face another invasion of Italy if they did not anticipate Philip's action. When the Assembly finally gave its approval, one of the Roman ambassadors whom the Senate had already sent to Greece to threaten

Philip and encourage his opponents presented the formal declaration of war to the king, who was at that time engaged in the siege of Abydos on the Hellespont, whereupon the conflict began. In accordance with their instructions the ambassadors then visited Antiochus in Syria, perhaps to intercede on behalf of Egypt or to assure him of the good will of Rome so that he might not abandon his Syrian campaign and unite his forces with those of Philip in Macedonia. Roman diplomacy leading up to the war shows that at this stage of her history Rome took states unilaterally under her protection without the formality of a treaty and tended to regard her friends not as equals but as clients.

The Second Macedonian War

Late in 200 a Roman army under the consul Sulpicius Galba crossed into Illyricum and tried to penetrate into Macedonia. Both in this and in the succeeding year, however, the Romans, although aided by the Aetolian Confederacy, Pergamon, Rhodes, and Athens, were unable to inflict any decisive defeat upon Philip or to invade his kingdom.

With the arrival of one of the consuls of 198, Titus Flamininus, the situation speedily changed. The Achaean Confederacy was won over to the side of Rome, and Flamininus succeeded in forcing Philip to evacuate Epirus and to withdraw into Thessaly. In the following winter negotiations for peace were opened. At the insistence of her Greek allies, Rome now demanded not merely a guarantee that Philip would refrain from attacking the Hellenes but also the evacuation of Corinth, Chalcis, and Demetrias, three fortresses known as "the fetters of Greece." Philip refused to make this concession.

The next year military operations were resumed with both armies in Thessaly. Early in the summer a battle was fought on a ridge of hills called Cynoscephalae (the Dogs' Heads), where the Romans won a complete victory. Although the Aetolians rendered valuable assistance in this engagement, the Macedonian defeat was due primarily to the superior flexibility of the Roman legionary formation over the phalanx. Philip fled to Macedonia and sued for peace. The Aetolians and his enemies in Greece sought his destruction, but

Flamininus realized the importance of Macedonia to the Greek world as a bulwark against the Celtic peoples of the lower Danube and would not support their demands. The terms fixed by the Roman Senate were: autonomy of the Hellenes, in Greece and Asia; evacuation of the Macedonian possessions in Greece, in the Aegean, and in Illyricum; an indemnity of 1,000 talents; and the surrender of nearly all his warships. These conditions Philip was obliged to accept (196). Soon afterwards he became a Roman ally.

At the Isthmian games of the same year Flamininus proclaimed the complete autonomy of the peoples who had been subject to Macedonia. The announcement provoked a tremendous outburst of enthusiasm among most of the Greek states. After spending some time in effecting this policy and in settling the claims of various states, Flamininus returned to Italy in 194, leaving the Greeks to make what use they would of their freedom. The dramatic proclamation of Flamininus is often attributed to the cultural philhellenism [admiration for Greek culture] increasingly noticeable at this time among the Roman ruling class. Rome's interest in Greek freedom was not sentimental, but was rather the natural result of political and strategic considerations growing out of the recent war. Rome was now merely applying throughout Greece a policy that she had previously used in Messana, Saguntum and Illyria. If the Greeks were free, from the Roman point of view they enjoyed the freedom of client states, which, as a matter of course, would pursue a foreign policy compatible with Roman interests and which would form a bulwark against any hostile action on the part of Philip or Antiochus.

Antiochus and the Aetolians Stir Up Trouble

Even before Flamininus and his army had withdrawn from Greece, the activities of Antiochus had awakened the mistrust of the Roman Senate and threatened hostilities. The Syrian king had completed the conquest of Lower Syria in 198. Profiting by the difficulties in which Philip of Macedon was involved, he had then turned his attention toward Asia Minor and Thrace with the hope of recovering the possessions once held by his ancestor, Seleucus I. The Romans were at the time too much occupied to oppose him. Outwardly he professed to be a friend of Rome and to be limiting his activities to the reestablishment of his empire's former extent. Eventually, in 196 he crossed over into Europe and took Thrace. The Romans tried to induce him to withdraw but were unsuccessful. Two years later Antiochus himself opened negotiations with the Senate to secure Roman recognition of his claims to Thrace and to certain cities in Asia Minor which, relying upon Roman support, refused to acknowledge his overlordship. The Roman government, cynically enough, was willing to abandon its self-proclaimed status as protector of the Greeks in Asia if Antiochus would evacuate Thrace. Since Antiochus, although harboring no designs against Rome, refused to be forced out of his European possessions, he decided to support the anti-Roman elements in Greece to force Rome to yield the points at issue. Accordingly, he willingly received deputations from the Aetolians, who were the leading opponents of Rome among the Greeks.

The Aetolians, Rome's allies in the war just concluded and greatly exaggerating the importance of their services, were disgruntled because Macedonia had not been entirely dismembered and they had been restrained from enlarging the territory of the Confederacy at the expense of their neighbors. In short, they wished to replace Macedonia as the leading Greek state. Accustomed to regard war as a legitimate source of revenue, they did not easily reconcile themselves to Rome's imposition of peace in Hellas. Ever since the battle of Cynoscephalae they had striven to undermine Roman influence among the Greeks, and now they sought to draw Antiochus into conflict with Rome.

In 192 they brought matters to a head by unexpectedly attacking some of Rome's supporters in Greece and seizing the fortress of Demetrias, which they offered to the king [Antiochus], to whom they also made an unauthorized promise of aid from Macedonia. Trusting in the support promised by the Aetolians, Antiochus sailed to Greece with an advance force of 10,000 men. Upon his arrival the Aetolians elected him their commander in chief. . . .

The Defeat of Antiochus

In 191 a Roman army under the consul Acilius Glabrio appeared in Greece and defeated the forces of Antiochus at Thermopylae. The king fled to Asia. Contrary to his hopes he had found little support in Greece. Philip of Macedon and the Achaean Confederacy adhered to the Romans, and the Aetolians were made helpless by an invasion of their own country. The Rhodians and Eumenes, the new king of Pergamon, joined their navies to the Roman fleet.

As Antiochus would not listen to the peace terms laid down by the Romans, the latter resolved to invade Asia Minor. Two naval victories, won with the aid of Rhodes and Pergamon, secured control of the Aegean, and in 190 a Roman force crossed the Hellespont. For commander the Senate had wished to designate Scipio Africanus, the greatest Roman general. As he had recently been consul he was now ineligible for that office. The law was circumvented by election of his brother Lucius to the consulate and his assignment to the command, and by the appointment of Publius to accompany him, apparently as a legate. This arrangement permitted Publius to assume practical direction of the campaign.

One decisive victory over Antiochus at Magnesia [in western Asia Minor] in the autumn of 190 brought him to terms. He agreed to surrender all territory north of the Taurus mountains and west of Pamphylia, to give up his war elephants, to surrender all but ten of his ships of war, to pay an indemnity of 15,000 talents in twelve annual instalments, and to abstain from attacking the allies of Rome. . . . He was still at liberty to defend himself if attacked. Peace upon these conditions was formally ratified in 188. This time Rome did not "free" all the Greeks as she had done in 196, since such an action would have produced too many petty states and future imbroglios [entanglements]. Some of the Greek city-states did receive their freedom, but Rhodes and Pergamon were the principal beneficiaries of the peace, which brought them an accession of territory at the expense of neighboring Greeks and non-Greeks alike. . . .

The Roman campaign of 191 against the Aetolians had caused the latter, who were also attacked by Philip of Macedon, to seek terms. The Romans demanded unconditional surrender, and the Aetolians decided to continue the struggle. No energetic measures were taken against them at once, but in 189 the consul Fulvius Nobilior pressed the war vigorously and besieged their chief stronghold, Ambracia. Since the obstinate resistance of its defenders defied all his efforts and since the Athenians were trying to act as mediators in ending the war, the Romans abandoned their demand for unconditional surrender. The Aetolians proved that they had not understood the meaning of clientship, and the Romans were determined that any peace treaty with them should express their dependent status. Peace was finally made on the following conditions: the Aetolian Confederacy was granted a permanent alliance with Rome on an unequal footing, with the obligation to support Rome against all her enemies; the Confederacy gave up all territory captured by its enemies during the war; Ambracia was surrendered and sacked. . . .

Although by her alliance with the Aetolians Rome had planted herself permanently on Greek soil and in the war with Antiochus had claimed to exercise a protectorate over the Greek world, the Senate as yet gave no indication of reversing the policy of Flamininus, and the Greek states remained friends of Rome in the enjoyment of political "independence." It was not long, however, before these friendly relations became seriously strained and Rome was induced to embark upon a policy of political and then military interference in Greek affairs, which ultimately put an end to the apparent freedom of Hellas.

Mainland Greece Falls Under Roman Control

Max Cary

In the fateful year 146 B.C., the Romans destroyed not only the once great city of Carthage, but also the Greek city of Corinth, located near the narrow land-bridge separating southern from central mainland Greece. Corinth's demise marked the conclusion of Rome's military campaigns in Greece. It also brought the Romans virtual control of the eastern Mediterranean sphere, complementing their mastery of the sea's western sector. The following account of the last few years of liberty for the inhabitants of mainland Greece (including Macedonia) is by the late, distinguished University of Michigan scholar Max Cary. He begins with the resistance offered to Rome by Macedonia's new king, Perseus, son of Philip V (who had signed a treaty with the Romans after they had defeated him in 197 B.C.). Cary then gives an overview of the main events of the Third Macedonian War (171–168 B.C.), including a very clear description of the pivotal battle of Pydna, and goes on to chronicle the demise of the Achaean League (a Greek alliance of cities similar to the Aetolian Confederacy). Finally, he describes the unfortunate end of Corinth, which left Rome as the single remaining "superpower" in the Mediterranean.

Philip's successor Perseus inherited the cautious temperament of the true Antigonid breed, but was trained in the self-assertive traditions of his father. His early policy was an unsteady compromise between these conflicting tendencies. At the outset of his reign he conciliated the [Roman] Senate by

---

Excerpted from *History of the Greek World from 323 to 146 B.C.* by Max Cary (London: Methuen,1963). Reprinted by permission of Routledge.

161

applying for a renewal of his father's treaty, and to the Greek cities in his dominions he was more considerate than Philip. But he placed himself in a false position by his ostentatious promises to bankrupts and political outlaws from the towns of the Greek Homeland. These appeals to the political and economic underworld brought him no solid support, while to the Romans they appeared as an attempt to overthrow their settlement of Greek affairs. Renewed visits by senatorial commissions, before whom Perseus failed to clear himself, gave rise in turn to fresh accusations from the king's malevolent neighbours. In 172 [B.C.] king Eumenes of Pergamum made a journey to Rome to present a crime-sheet against Perseus. Returning home by way of Delphi, he was all but killed by a falling rock from [Mount] Parnassus [near Delphi, in central Greece], and he used this incident—which may quite well have been due to natural causes—to pillory the Macedonian king as an assassin. Hereupon the Senate resolved its doubts by sending an order to disarm as an ultimatum to Perseus, and thus virtually forced on the Third Macedonian War. Like the Third Punic War, this conflict was the outcome of ill-defined suspicions rather than of clearly proved guilt.

The Fall of Macedonia

The Third Macedonian War was a plain trial of strength between Macedon and Rome. Perseus received no Greek support save from a few minor towns of Boeotia. The Epirotes [inhabitants of the kingdom of Epirus] declared themselves sufficiently to draw Roman vengeance upon their country, but gave Perseus no effectual aid. The abstention of the Greeks was partly due to Perseus' parsimony [stinginess], which deterred him from spending the accumulated funds of the Macedonian treasury in a timely diplomatic offensive. But it is highly unlikely that he could have bought many Greek states for a war against Rome. Apart from the Greek exiles and debtors, he had on his side some political leaders who chafed at the inevitable restrictions entailed with Rome's gift of freedom to the Greeks. But the governing classes in general acquiesced in [gave in to] a Roman suzerainty [domination] which greatly added to their security, and they had not forgotten Cynoscephalæ [the battle in which the Romans had decisively defeated Philip V]. Under these conditions a general Greek rally to Macedon was out of the question. On the other hand Perseus had scrupulously avoided those blunders of policy which had brought the Greeks into the field against Philip. The Romans therefore received no Greek assistance except from the Achæan League, which supplied a small contingent, and from Pergamum and Rhodes, which furnished a few warships and transports. Their total field force, numbering some 35,000, hardly exceeded that of Perseus.

The Romans and Perseus, having fumbled into war, spent three years in trying to fumble out of it. Though the Roman generals had a fleet at their disposal, they derived scarcely any benefit from it. For two years they made vain endeavours to force the Olympus range between Thessaly and Macedonia. In 169 the consul Marcius Philippus carried the barrier, but more by luck than by management. On the other hand Perseus' congenital cautiousness recovered possession of him on the field of battle. A victory gained by him in a cavalry action near Larissa in 171 frightened him into making two successive attempts at negotiation, and in 169 he abandoned the Olympus position before the Romans had extricated [removed] their columns from the mountain defiles. It was not until 168 that the Roman army and fleet, brought into effective co-operation by the consul Æmilius Paullus, were able to acquire a definite foothold in Macedonia.

In 168, however, the war was decided in the course of a few minutes. The battle of Pydna, in which Perseus' army was virtually annihilated, was in essentials a replica of Cynoscephalæ. Developing by chance from an affair of outposts, it began with a mass attack by the Macedonian phalanx, which Paullus, a seasoned veteran, declared to have been the most terrifying sight in his ample experience. The Roman legions, which never proved their elasticity and manoeuvring power more brilliantly than on this field, fell back in good order upon higher ground, and as the momentum of the charging phalanx dislocated its ranks, they thrust themselves, company by company, into its gaps or round its flanks. The Macedonian infantry, unable to reform its line, and left unprotected by its mounted flank guards, was quickly killed off in a veritable battue.

Macedonia Dismembered, Epirus Desolated

During the Third Macedonian War anti-Roman feeling among the Greeks had been strengthened by the failure of the earlier Roman commanders to protect the civilian population against marauding troops and by their own excessive requisitions. But Greek resentment was allayed by the exemplary discipline enforced by Paullus upon his soldiery. Besides, the massacre of Pydna relieved the Romans of all further reason for fearing the Greeks. Nevertheless the generosity . . . with which the Senate had hitherto treated Greek affairs now gave way to anxious suspicion. Though for the third time they left the Greeks free and withdrew their troops, they took precautions, wise and unwise, against future misuse of their liberty. In Macedonia they dethroned the Antigonid dynasty and set up four federal republics extending in a line from the Illyrian frontier to the river Nestus. The new federations were in themselves a justifiable experiment, for the growth of town life in Macedon had made the people ripe for a measure of self-government. Moreover, in fixing the yearly rate of war-indemnity at a mere half of the former royal land-tax, they left Macedon in a better financial position than under the Antigonids. But in prohibiting all intercourse, political or economic, between the four succession-states, they violated the legitimate sense of nationhood among the Macedonians; and in deporting to Italy not only Perseus but all the royal officials they left the republics without political leadership.

In Greece the Romans made no alterations in the governments and but few changes in the frontiers. But they took strong measures to purge the cities of declared or suspected sympathizers with Macedon. In Ætolia they furnished troops to their principal supporters, who executed five hundred antagonists after a farcical trial. In Achæa, where a party led by Lycortas and his son Polybius (the future historian) had unsuccessfully advocated neutrality, they first demanded a judicial massacre on the Ætolian pattern; on discovering that they could not carry this point they deported one thousand suspects . . . under pretence of arranging for their trial in Italy. In Epirus the ex-consul Paullus was bidden to punish the ineffective sympathies of the people for

The Romans Level Corinth

This is the brief description of the Roman destruction of Corinth provided by the second-century A.D. Greek writer Pausanias in his travel book, the Guide to Greece *(Peter Levi's translation).*

The Achaians who escaped to Corinth after the battle ran away during that night, and many of the Corinthians fled at the same time. Mummius held back from entering Corinth even though the gates were open, suspecting there might be an ambush inside the walls, but two days after the battle he took possession in force and burnt Corinth. Most of the people who were left there were murdered by the Romans, and Mummius auctioned the women and children. He auctioned the slaves as well, those of them I mean who were set free and fought beside the Achaians, and were not killed at once in the fighting. He collected the most marvellous of sacred dedications and works of art, and gave the less important things to Attalos's general Philopoimen: and in my time at Pergamon they still had the spoils of Corinth. Mummius broke down the walls and confiscated the armaments of every city that had fought against the Romans even before Rome sent out its advisory commission, and when his commissioners arrived he put an end to the democracies and established government by property qualification. Greece was taxed and the monied classes were barred from the acquisition of property abroad. All national leagues alike were put an end to, Achaian and Phokian or Boiotian or anywhere. . . .

At this time more than any other, Greece sank into the last stages of weakness: crippled and utterly devastated from the beginning in this part or that by a daemonic spirit.

Pausanias, *Guide to Greece.* 2 vols. Trans. Peter Levi. New York: Penguin Books, 1971, vol. 1, pp. 266–68.

Perseus with a systematic dragonade [persecution] in which he carried off 150,000 souls to the Roman slave-market. This utterly inexcusable brutality, which left Epirus half-desolate, was never requited [avenged] upon the Romans. Their more venial mistakes in Macedon and Achæa brought their revenge with them.

The Fourth Macedonian War

In Macedon the new federations so far proved their capacity to govern, that in 158 B.C. the Senate removed some of the previous commercial embargoes. But the restriction of intercourse between the four republics prevented their taking adequate measures for common defence. By a fortunate chance the Dardanians [neighboring Balkan tribesmen], having recently been engaged in a murderous war in the Balkan hinterland, were slow to seize their opportunity. But in 150 an adventurer named Andriscus, who claimed to be a son of Perseus, won enough adherents to gain successive battles against the . . . levies [troops] on either side of the river Strymon [running through central Macedonia]. From a reunited Macedon the pretender mustered sufficient troops to defeat a small Roman force which the Senate hastily sent against him. But his improvised levies were easily disposed of by an augmented Roman army under Cæcilius Metellus (148), and Macedon made its final surrender to Rome. After the Fourth Macedonian War the Senate did not repeat the mistake of partitioning Macedon, yet it dared not entrust the entire country to a native administration. It therefore broke with its long-standing policy of leaving Greek lands ungarrisoned and converted Macedon into a Roman province. By this act it virtually closed the book of Macedonian history.

The Achæan League Rebels

In Peloponnesus the deportations of the Achæan suspects, far from cowing the League, drove it to open hostility against Rome. For sixteen years the Senate turned a deaf ear to the League's protests against the detention of its citizens; in 151 it released without trial the surviving remnant of the prisoners. But this act of grace came too late to appease Achæan resentment. Since the Third Macedonian War the revolutionary element, whose chief strength lay in the proletariate of Corinth, had gained steadily upon the friends of Rome and of domestic peace. . . . The stalwarts of the League fixed a fresh quarrel upon Sparta over the thorny question of its special privileges, and thus provoked a direct conflict with the Senate, to which the Spartans as usual carried their complaints. The extremist leader Diæus prepared a military execution upon Sparta without awaiting the Senate's decision, which was delayed through its preoccupation with the Macedonian and the Punic Wars. The Senate eventually answered his contumacy [stubbornness] with an order to the Achæans to restore full independence to Sparta, which desired it, and to Corinth and Argos, who had no wish to secede. With this sentence of mutilation it finally threw the League into the hands of the extremists, and the Senate's envoys barely escaped death at the hands of the Corinthian mob. In 147 the Senate endeavoured to re-open negotiations by tacitly rescinding its previous instructions, while Metellus sent a conciliatory message from Macedon. But the new Achæan general Critolaus, mistaking the Senate's overture for a confession of weakness, played off its commissioner with impudent chicanery [trickery], and the mob of Corinth hooted Metellus' envoys off the platform. To cut off the League's retreat, Critolaus had himself proclaimed dictator by tumultuary procedure. With his usurped powers he compelled the wealthier citizens to contribute heavy taxes and to set free a quota of slaves for military service; and in 146 he directed an expedition against Heracleia-ad-Œtam [a town near the pass of Thermopylæ, in central Greece], which had under unknown circumstances been annexed to the League, but had profited by the Senate's recent pronouncement to re-assert its independence. He was joined on the way by contingents from Thebes and other Central Greek towns, where the party of social revolution was in the ascendant. But while he lay before Heracleia he was taken unawares by Metellus, who put the Achæan forces to headlong rout and flung them right back upon Corinth. Meanwhile Diæus had collected a second forced levy of freemen and slaves, amounting to some 15,000 men. With this scratch force he offered a desperate resistance to Metellus' successor Mummius, who had brought up large Roman reinforcements. In a battle on the Isthmus [of Corinth, the narrow land bridge connecting the Peloponnesus to the Greek mainland] the raw Achæan levies proved once more—if proof were needed—that Greeks under firm leadership could fight without flinching; but in the face of hopeless odds they met with irretrievable defeat.

The End of Greek Liberty

In Greece, as in Macedon, the Senate decided to take no further chances. By way of upholding the sanctity of ambassadors, it ordered the inhabitants of Corinth to be sold into slavery, and the town to be levelled to the ground. It dissolved the Achæan League and annexed its component states to the province of Macedonia. These states henceforth paid tribute to Rome and in some cases had their constitutions remodelled. Athens retained its full freedom; the small local leagues in which the states of Central Greece and Thessaly had been grouped by previous Roman action retained their autonomy under the supervision of the governor of Macedonia. Under this settlement the Greek ideal of local autonomy was in large measure realized, and for the first time in its history the country enjoyed an enduring peace. But the ideal of a United States of Greece was finally shattered, and the era of liberty and of fertile political experiment in Greek lands gave way to two thousand years of forced inertia.

Rome Absorbs and Is Transformed by Greek Culture

L.P. Wilkinson

A great irony of the final stage of Rome's rise to supremacy in the Mediterranean world—the defeat and absorption of the Greeks—was that the conquerors were profoundly transformed by the conquered. The Romans were for a long time mostly conservative, austere, culturally backward farmers and soldiers. And when they came into contact with Greek customs and ideas, especially artistic and architectural styles and philosophic concepts, they were mightily impressed by them. The result, as explained here by L.P. Wilkinson, of King's College, Cambridge, was that beginning in the third and second centuries B.C. Rome became philhellenic and adopted many aspects of Greek culture. (Philhellenism is a fascination or love for Greek culture, since the term Hellenism means Greek civilization.) And this process continued, eventually producing the Greco-Roman cultural synthesis later ages came to call "classical civilization." Wilkinson supports his discussion with references to Magna Graecia, the collective term for the Greek cities of southern Italy that were eventually absorbed by Rome; the third-century B.C. Roman playwright Plautus, who copied the characters and conventions of Greek comedy; the Greek historian Polybius, whom the Romans took as a hostage when they conquered Greece, but who came to be thoroughly Romanized; and the first-century-B.C. Roman epic poet Virgil (or Vergil), whose personality and writings were shaped by and steeped in Greek culture.

Excerpted from *The Roman Experience* by L.P. Wilkinson (Lanham, MD: University Press of America). Copyright © 1974 by Random House, Inc. Used with permission from Random House, Inc.

The cultural history of Rome became progressively the history of her transfiguration through contact with Greek ideas. Legend apart, she was early a debtor to Greece through [the Etruscans]. . . . Through them came the Greek alphabet, vines and olives, bronzes and ceramics, and crafts of war. Rome . . . resembled a Greek polis with her acropolis (the Capitol), her agora (the Comitia), and her boule (the Senate). [The fourth-century B.C. Greek philosopher] Heraclides Ponticus, writing of Rome's temporary capture by the Gauls in 390, referred to her as a Greek city. . . .

Religion

Indeed Greek influence was particularly felt in the sphere of religion. The old Roman religion of spirits (*numina*) was largely impersonal. Even the sex of some deities remained uncertain. But other gods were early imported. Minerva, from Etruscan Falerii, formed a triad on the Capitol with Jupiter and Juno [the Rome equivalent of Hera, Zeus's wife]. Some newcomers, absorbed as Rome's influence spread, were admitted even into the *pomerium*, the sacred heart of the city—Hercules, for instance, and the twins Castor and Pollux, who came from Tusculum. The gods were still largely functional, names with little personality attached. But Hercules, connected with trade, was certainly the Greek Herakles, and the twin gods were the Greek Kastor and Polydeukes. The more the Romans came to know about the Greeks, the more they sought to identify their gods with Greek gods. Thus Jupiter the sky god could clearly be equated with Zeus; Minerva the handicraft goddess, with Athena. The Greek Olympians were far from impersonal: they were a family with all the passions and experiences of humans. So first by word of mouth, and later through literature and art, the Romans acquired what they had lacked before, a rich mythology. Yet the old *numina* had been impressive for their very impalpability, and gods with human form and all too human biographies, though at first easier to deal with, were eventually to prove less credible.

Another Greek import destined to be of great influence was the Sibylline Books, which reputedly came from the old

Greek colony of Cumae, north of Neapolis. In fact all importations of Greek deities were initiated by these Books—Demeter, Dionysus, and Persephone (under the names of Ceres, Liber, and Libera) as early as the beginning of the fifth century—though the Senate kept a tight control of their prerogatives. The Books were kept secret in the Temple of Jupiter by a permanent Board of Ten, who consulted them by order of the Senate in times of crisis. . . . When Roman armies first crossed into Greece in the second century, their commanders made offerings at Greek shrines, giving an example to their troops, and thus senatorial control was loosened. . . .

Poetry and Plays

Until the middle years of the third century the Hellenization of Rome had progressed gradually and perhaps imperceptibly. It now gathered pace. In the words of [noted modern historian Theodor] Mommsen (*History of Rome*), "The Romans began to feel the lack of a richer intellectual life, and to be startled, as it were, by their own utter lack of mental culture." In the twenty-three years of the First Punic War many Romans saw service in Magna Graecia, including the cultural centers of Sicily. It is significant that the first Roman Festival after victory was won, in 240, included as a supplement to the circus races the novelty of Greek plays, a tragedy and a comedy, in Latin versions composed by Livius Andronicus, a teacher of Greek origin who had been freed from slavery by his master. If it is true, as one tradition asserts, that he was brought to Rome as a small boy among the thirty thousand captive slaves from Tarentum in 272, then he must have acquired at Rome not only his mastery of Latin but his Greek culture, in a milieu of Greek slaves and immigrants. These plays, and his translation of the *Odyssey* . . . really inaugurated written Latin literature. . . . They also inaugurated translation as a European art transcending mere word-for-word rendering. The astonishingly rapid development of Latin literature was due to his pioneering enterprise. He had to select or coin a poetic diction, match Greek words with Latin, and recognize and develop the peculiar potentialities of the language. His *Odyssey* was read in schools for at least two centuries. . . . We have the titles of eight or nine of his tragedies. They suggest that he went back beyond the Hellenistic tragedians to the great ones of the fifth century. If so, this was in itself a signal service. . . .

Hard on his heels came a greater genius, Naevius—the only one of the early poets to be born a Roman citizen—outspoken, full of "Campanian pride" and the new Romano-Italian patriotism. He is best known for his epic . . . on the First Punic War, into which he inserted the story of Aeneas' coming to Rome from Troy by way of Dido's Carthage. Representing Rome as founded by the will of the gods, this South Italian presaged . . . Vergil, in recognizing the Romans as a people with a mission. But he also wrote plays, not only versions of Greek ones to rival those of Livius, whom he surpassed especially in comedy, but original ones on Roman subjects. . . .

Plautus further familiarized the Romans with Greek meters and with the ever-popular New Comedy of fourth-century Athens. Plays were connected with religious festivals, of which several new ones had been established during the Second Punic War. The world of New Comedy was a gay one in which, for instance, young men, abetted by sympathetic slaves, deceived their fathers in their pursuit of glamorous courtesans [prostitutes], whom they could not however legally marry until, in the denouement [conclusion], the girl turned out to be freeborn after all. Plautus introduced odd references to Roman institutions that amused, as anachronisms do, by their incongruity; and a great deal of Roman spirit. But the audience thoroughly understood that this was a Greek world, a world of temporary escape from the moral restraints of normal life. He could not, however, make a courtesan an idealized human being. . . . That would have been too much for the matrons of Rome in his day. And occasional hints suggest that he has a mild contempt for this Greek way of life and expects to carry his audience with him. *Pergraecari* was the word—"to be ever so Greek."

This was in the time of Scipio Africanus. In the next generation, in the time of Aemilius Paullus, there appeared in the circle of his son Scipio, then barely twenty years of age, an

African slave who acquired on manumission the name Terentius. The six plays of Terence, though not slavish imitations, are conscious efforts to reproduce far more nearly the spirit, style, and appurtenances of Greek New Comedy. The Hellenization of Rome had in fact proceeded so far that instead of having Greek comedies adapted for the Roman stage simply because there were no others available, as by Plautus, the object had become to put on something as Greek as possible. Plautus was out to make his audience laugh. Terence was more interested in presenting them with problems of complex situations and drawing subtle characterizations. . . .

Visual Arts

The visual arts also began to penetrate the consciousness of Romans in the third century. The first occasion was the Triumph in 272 of Lucius Papirius Cursor, captor of Tarentum, when statues and pictures were among the treasures displayed. Two thousand statues were carried off from the Etruscan city of Volsinii in 265. When Marcellus took Syracuse in 211 he flooded Rome with works of art looted from temples as well as secular buildings. By contrast, Fabius, when he retook Tarentum two years later, pointedly brought back one statue only, the Hercules of Lysippus, as a religious trophy; for already a group was forming in reaction against the craze for Greek things. But the tide could not be turned when the Romans became involved in the Greek mainland in the next century. Marcus Fulvius, returning after his successful campaign against the Aetolians in 187, founded a temple of Hercules and the Muses, adorning it with statues including a famous group of the Nine. The loot at his Triumph included 785 bronze and 250 marble statues. For the games that he celebrated for ten days many Greek performers were imported, and athletes as well as wild beasts were for the first time seen at a spectacle in Rome. All the royal treasure of Macedon graced the Triumph of Aemilius Paullus in 167. Rome was beginning to realize that leisure (*otium*) could be consciously cultivated as well as business (*negotium*).

In architecture the colonnade, that feature of leisurely Hellenistic life, was first introduced to Rome for the Empo-

rium constructed between 193 and 174 in the wharf quarter.
. . . It was not until 146 that marble was first used for building at Rome. Concrete, with all its potential for the
grandiose, made its appearance about 120. We have no
means of tracing by what stages the domestic architecture, a
blend of Hellenistic and Italian such as we find in the House
of the Faun at Pompeii, took hold of the capital. . . . Servius
Sulpicius Galba in the second century had a pavilion with a
pyramidal roof in his grounds, separate from his atrium net-
work, for purposes of secluded study. Many of the architects
were imported Greeks. But one Roman at least became distinguished internationally, Cossutius, invited by Antiochus
IV of Syria to redesign the temple of Zeus Olympios at
Athens, whose completion he had undertaken to finance.

Little attempt, however, was made to develop a Roman visual art analogous to Roman poetry, though the tragic poet
Pacuvius was also a painter. Nor must we suppose that the
citizens, either senators or commoners, acquired quickly or
uniformly a true appreciation of Greek art. When in 167
Lucius Anicius produced at his triumph four of the best oboe
players in Greece, neither he nor the audience had any idea
what to expect, and a scene of the wildest farce ensued. In
115 reactionary censors banned all musical instruments except the Italian oboe. But at least a respect for art spread.
Mummius, who took nothing for himself from the sack of
Corinth in 146, marked his censorship four years later by
presenting captured works of art to communities of the
Roman commonwealth as far afield as Italica in Spain and
Parma in the Po Valley. Corinthian bronzes became show-
pieces of many Roman houses.

Philosophy

But it was in the realm of ideas that Greece made most impact
on Rome. . . . The more educated . . . probably had recourse
to Pythagoreanism. Pythagoras was the great sage of Magna
Graecia, a name to reckon with three hundred years after his
death. Legend had it, anachronistically, that he had instructed
Numa, the king to whom the Roman religious calendar was
attributed. When, at a crisis in the Samnite Wars, the Delphic

Oracle told the Romans to erect a statue to "the wisest of the Greeks," the Senate put its money on Pythagoras.

The chief Pythagorean doctrine was that of the reincarnations of the soul (which was separable from the incarcerating body). . . . In 181 [B.C.] there was a strange affair. A minor official dug up on land of his at Rome two coffins. One, which was empty, bore the name of Numa. The other contained books written on suspiciously new-looking material purporting to be by Numa and dealing with the Pythagorean philosophy. They eventually came into the hands of the praetor, who pronounced them subversive of religion. He allowed the discoverer to appeal to the tribunes, who passed the buck to the Senate; and the Senate authorized the praetor to burn them publicly. One can only suppose that their offense was "putting ideas into people's heads." . . .

In 161 the Senate authorized the praetor to expel philosophers and rhetoricians [teachers of oratory]. The inclusion of the latter suggests that the offense was not propounding any specific doctrine but causing people to waste time. . . .

The fact was that from contact with Greece the Romans were rapidly passing through a development in thought that had taken her three centuries. This was particularly so as regards belief in the old gods. For educated people in the Hellenistic world, such as Polybius, this belief had been superseded by philosophy, mainly rationalistic. Such rationalism did not preclude some form of belief in the existence of one god; and many vaguely believed in a power they called Tyche, in Latin Fortuna, which was something more than a personification of mere chance. We begin to hear stories of skepticism. Claudius Pulcher at Drepanum in 249 threw the sacred chickens into the sea with the words "If they won't eat, let them drink" (their not eating was a bad omen). Marcellus nullified what would have been bad omens if he had observed them by the simple device of drawing the curtains of his litter. . . . One symptom was a growing difficulty in getting citizens to take on priesthoods that involved irksome restrictions. [The Roman writer] Ennius contributed by retailing the work of the Alexandrian Euhemerus, who maintained that the gods were mortals deified by man for their services. . . .

Rome Captivated by Greece

[By the time that Polybius settled down in Rome in 145 B.C., he, like some other Greeks, had come gudgingly to admire the Romans, despite Rome's recent subjugation of Greece. Thereafter, as Greek and Roman cultures continued to merge, the two peoples maintained a sort of love-hate relationship. Polybius] ends his history with an expression of gratitude for concessions Rome made at his instigation in recognition of his good will and prays that this relationship may remain for his lifetime. Despite her treatment of his fellow hostages, he was devoted to her. He disapproved of radical governments and, like some modern imperialists, he could not understand how any people could prefer to be misgoverned by unscrupulous leaders of their own rather than enjoy greater security and welfare under the protection of a foreign power. . . . And yet he let slip a melancholy remark: "The destruction of Carthage is considered to be one of the greatest calamities. But perished Carthage has no memories: Greece lives on to remember her past happiness." Greek opinion, according to him, was divided. Some said Rome was only sensible to destroy her rival; some produced legalistic excuses for her; but some said she had no excuse. . . .

More than a century later [the Roman satirist] Juvenal was to exclaim testily, "Romans, I cannot bear the city gone Greek." Yet it was primarily her willingness to respond to Hellenism that made Rome normative, largely for good, in Western civilization. Along with what was both sound and decadent in contemporary Greece she absorbed through literature something of the spirit of the great classical age of the fifth and fourth centuries. . . . In historical reality, as [the Roman poet] Horace put it, "captive Greece captivated her barbarous conqueror."

Appendix of Documents

Document 1: Victory for the Father of the Roman Race

The ancient Romans came to see their history as beginning with the arrival of the Trojan prince Aeneas in Italy and his subsequent establishment of the family line that led to the founders of the city of Rome. Aeneas supposedly defeated an indigenous Italian people, the Rutulians, led by the warrior Turnus. Aeneas's personal victory over Turnus, described in this excerpt from an excellent recent translation of Virgil's Aeneid *by David West, foreshadowed Rome's later defeat of other Italian peoples in its rise to mastery of the whole peninsula.*

Aeneas kept pressing his pursuit with his huge spear flashing, as long as a tree, and these were the words he spoke in his anger: 'What is the delay now? Why are you still shirking, Turnus? This is not a race! It is a fight with dangerous weapons at close quarters. Turn yourself into any shape you like. Scrape together all your resources of spirit and skill. Pray to sprout wings and fly to the stars of heaven, or shut yourself up and hide in a hole in the ground!' Turnus replied, shaking his head: 'You are fierce, Aeneas, but wild words do not frighten me. It is the gods that cause me to fear, the gods and the enmity of Jupiter.' He said no more but looked round and saw a huge rock, a huge and ancient rock which happened to be lying on the plain, a boundary stone put there to settle a dispute about land. Twelve picked men like those the earth now produces could scarcely lift it up on to their shoulders, but he caught it up in his trembling hands and, rising to his full height and running at speed, he hurled it at his enemy. But he had no sense of running or going, of lifting or moving the huge rock. His knees gave way. His blood chilled and froze and the stone rolled away under its own impetus over the open ground between them, but it did not go the whole way and it did not strike its target. Just as when we are asleep, when in the weariness of night, rest lies heavy on our eyes, we dream we are trying desperately to run further and not succeeding, till we fall exhausted in the middle of our efforts; the tongue is useless; the strength we know we have, fails our body; we have no voice, no words to obey our will—so it was with Turnus. Wherever his courage sought a way, the dread goddess barred his progress. During these moments, the thoughts whirled in his brain. He gazed at the Rutulians and the city. He faltered with fear.

He began to tremble at the death that was upon him. He could see nowhere to run, no way to come at his enemy, no chariot anywhere, no sister to drive it.

As he faltered the deadly spear of Aeneas flashed. His eyes had picked the spot and he threw from long range with all his weight behind the throw. Stones hurled by siege artillery never roar like this. The crash of the bursting thunderbolt is not so loud. Like a dark whirlwind it flew carrying death and destruction with it. Piercing the outer rings of the sevenfold shield and laying open the lower rim of the breastplate, it went whistling through the middle of the thigh. When the blow struck, down went great Turnus, bending his knee to the ground. The Rutulians rose with a groan which echoed round the whole mountain, and far and wide the high forests sent back the sound of their voices. He lowered his eyes and stretched out his right hand to beg as a suppliant. 'I have brought this upon myself,' he said, 'and for myself I ask nothing. Make use of what Fortune has given you, but if any thought of my unhappy father can touch you, I beg of you—and you too had such a father in Anchises—take pity on the old age of Daunus, and give me back to my people, or if you prefer it, give them back my dead body. You have defeated me, and the men of Ausonia have seen me defeated and stretching out my hands to you. Lavinia is yours. Do not carry your hatred any further.'

There stood Aeneas, deadly in his armour, rolling his eyes, but he checked his hand, hesitating more and more as the words of Turnus began to move him, when suddenly his eyes caught the fatal baldric of the boy Pallas [one of Aeneas's followers] high on Turnus' shoulder with the glittering studs he knew so well. Turnus had defeated and wounded him and then killed him, and now he was wearing his belt on his shoulder as a battle honour taken from an enemy. Aeneas feasted his eyes on the sight of this spoil, this reminder of his own wild grief, then, burning with mad passion and terrible in his wrath, he cried: 'Are you to escape me now, wearing the spoils stripped from the body of those I loved? By this wound which I now give, it is Pallas who makes sacrifice of you. It is Pallas who exacts the penalty in your guilty blood.' Blazing with rage, he plunged the steel full into his enemy's breast. The limbs of Turnus were dissolved in cold and his life left him with a groan, fleeing in anger down to the shades [underworld].

Virgil, *Aeneid*. Trans. David West. New York: Penguin Books, 1990, pp. 330–32.

Document 2: Romulus Slays His Brother Remus

According to legend, among Aeneas's descendants were the twin brothers Romulus and Remus, who set out to establish a city. But as recounted here by the great first-century-B.C. Roman historian Livy, the brothers quarreled and Remus was killed, leaving Romulus to found the city alone and name it after himself. (In reality, the character, who was probably mythical, seems to have been named after the city, since the name Romulus likely means "the Roman.")

Romulus and Remus [after a successful struggle for recognition as rightful members of Alba Longa's royal house] . . . were suddenly seized by an urge to found a new settlement on the spot where they had been left to drown as infants and had been subsequently brought up. . . . Unhappily, the brothers' plans for the future were marred by . . . jealousy and ambition. A disgraceful quarrel arose from a matter in itself trivial. As the brothers were twins and all questions of seniority were therefore precluded, they determined to ask the gods of the countryside to declare by augury [omens, symbolic signs] which of them should govern the new town once it was founded, and give his name to it. . . . Remus, the story goes, was the first to receive a sign—six vultures; and no sooner was this made known to the people than double the number of birds appeared to Romulus. The followers of each promptly saluted their masters as king. . . . Angry words ensued, followed all too soon by blows, and in the course of the affray Remus was killed. There is another story, a commoner one, according to which Remus, by way of jeering at his brother, jumped over the half-built walls of the new settlement, whereupon Romulus killed him in a fit of rage, adding the threat, "So perish whoever else shall overleap my battlements." This, then, was how Romulus obtained the sole power. The newly built city was called by its founder's name.

Livy, *History of Rome*, excerpted in Bernard Knox, ed., *The Norton Book of Classical Literature*. New York: W.W. Norton, 1993, pp. 704–705.

Document 3: The Founder Organizes and Populates the Growing City

In this excerpt from his famous history of Rome, Livy passes on the traditions about how Romulus created the Senate from the heads of the Roman clans and then solved the problem of there being too few women in the city by kidnapping the women of a neighboring people, the Sabines. As told, these traditions are almost certainly legendary. However, they may be distorted memories of real events. The seizure of the Sabine women, for example, may recall one or more incidents in which Roman raiders captured large numbers of Sabines, including women, and brought them back to Rome.

Meanwhile Rome was growing. More and more ground was coming within the circuit of its walls. Indeed, the rapid expansion of the enclosed area was out of proportion to the actual population, and evidently indicated an eye to the future. In antiquity the founder of a new settlement, in order to increase its population, would as a matter of course shark up a lot of homeless and destitute folk and pretend that they were 'born of earth' to be his progeny; Romulus now followed a similar course: to help fill his big new town, he threw open, in the ground—now enclosed—between the two copses as you go up the Capitoline hill, a place of asylum for fugitives. Hither fled for refuge all the rag-tag-and-bobtail from the neighbouring peoples: some free, some slaves, and all of them wanting nothing but a fresh start. That mob was the first real addition to the City's strength, the first step to her future greatness.

Having now adequate numbers, Romulus proceeded to temper strength with policy and turned his attention to social organization. He created a hundred senators—fixing that number either because it was enough for his purpose, or because there were no more than a hundred who were in a position to be made 'Fathers', as they were called, or Heads of Clans. The title of 'fathers' (*patres*) undoubtedly was derived from their rank, and their descendants were called 'patricians'.

Rome was now strong enough to challenge any of her neighbours; but, great though she was, her greatness seemed likely to last only for a single generation. There were not enough women, and that, added to the fact that there was no intermarriage with neighbouring communities, ruled out any hope of maintaining the level of population. Romulus accordingly, on the advice of his senators, sent representatives to the various peoples across his borders to negotiate alliances and the right of intermarriage for the newly established state. The envoys were instructed to point out that cities, like everything else, have to begin small; in course of time, helped by their own worth and the favour of heaven, some, at least, grow rich and famous, and of these Rome would assuredly be one: Gods had blessed her birth, and the valour of her people would not fail in the days to come. The Romans were men, as they were; why, then, be reluctant to intermarry with them?

Romulus's overtures were nowhere favourably received; it was clear that everyone despised the new community, and at the same time feared, both for themselves and for posterity, the growth of this new power in their midst. More often than not his envoys were dismissed with the question of whether Rome had thrown open her doors to female, as well as to male, runaways and vagabonds, as that would evidently be the most suitable way for Romans to get wives. The young Romans naturally resented this jibe, and a clash seemed inevitable. Romulus, seeing it must come, set the scene for it with elaborate care. Deliberately hiding his resentment, he prepared to celebrate the Consualia, a solemn festival in honour of Neptune, patron of the horse, and sent notice of his intention all over the neighbouring countryside. The better to advertise it, his people lavished upon their preparations for the spectacle all the resources—such as they were in those days—at their command. On the appointed day crowds flocked to Rome, partly, no doubt, out of sheer curiosity to see the new town. The majority were from the neighbouring settlements of Caenina, Crustumium, and Antemnae, but all the Sabines were there too, with their wives and children. Many houses offered hospitable entertainment to the visitors; they were invited to inspect the fortifications, layout, and numerous buildings of the town, and expressed their surprise at the rapidity of its growth. Then the great moment came; the show began, and nobody had eyes or thoughts for anything else. This was the Romans' opportunity: at a given signal all the able-bodied men burst through the crowd and seized the young women. Most of the girls were the prize of whoever got hold of them first, but a few conspicuously handsome ones had been previously marked down for leading senators, and these were brought to their houses by special gangs. . . .

By this act of violence the fun of the festival broke up in panic. The girls' unfortunate parents made good their escape, not without bitter comments on the treachery of their hosts and heartfelt prayers to the God to whose festival they had come in all good faith in the solemnity of the occasion, only to be grossly deceived, The young women were no less indignant and as full of foreboding for the future.

Romulus, however, reassured them. Going from one to another he declared that their own parents were really to blame, in that they had been too proud to allow intermarriage with their neighbours; nevertheless, they need not fear; as married women they would share all the fortunes of Rome, all the privileges of the community, and they would be bound to their husbands by the dearest bond of all, their children. He urged them to forget their wrath and give their hearts to those to whom chance had given their bodies. Often, he said, a sense of injury yields in the end to affection, and their husbands would treat them all the more kindly in that they would try, each one of them, not only to fulfil their own part of the bargain but also to make up to their wives for the homes and parents they had lost. The men, too, played their part: they spoke honeyed words and vowed that it was passionate love which had prompted their offence. No plea can better touch a woman's heart.

Livy, *The History of Rome from Its Foundation.* Books 1–5 published as *Livy: The Early History of Rome.* Trans. Aubrey de Sélincourt. New York: Penguin Books, 1971, pp. 42–44.

Document 4: The Traditional Hard-working Roman Peasant Farmer

Whoever Rome's early leaders may have been and whatever policies they may have initiated, the Roman state was built on the backs of generation after generation of peasant farmers who were either poor or of moderate means. Throughout their long history, the Romans retained a strong nostalgia for the fields and countryside and a deep respect for the simplicity, austerity, honesty, and unselfish dedication of the traditional Roman farmer. This description of such a farmer comes from an anonymous ancient document titled Moretum. *(The term* moretum *is often translated as "salad," but more accurately describes a pesto sauce-like mixture of vegetables, herbs, oil, and sometimes cheese that was a common staple of the peasants.)*

And now night had completed twice five winter hours, and the winged sentry [the rooster] announced the new day with his crowing. Simulus, the peasant farmer of a meager little plot, worried about gnawing hunger on this coming day. He slowly raised his weary limbs from his ugly little cot. With anxious hand he groped through the stagnant darkness and felt his way to the fireplace, burning his hand when he touched it. One tiny spark remained from a burned log, but the ashes concealed the glow of live flames underneath. Stooping over, he moved his lamp forward, close to these embers, and drew out with a needle the dry wick. With frequent huffs and puffs, he stiffed up the sluggish fire. Finally, when the fire had caught and the lamp was lit, he turned away, using his hand to shield the wick light from a draft.

He unlocked the cupboard door with a key. Spread out on the cupboard floor was a paltry pile of grain. From this he took for himself as much as his measuring bucket held. He moved over to the mill and put his trusty lamp on a small shelf built onto the wall for the purpose. Then he slipped off his outer garment and, clad only in a shaggy goatskin, he swept the stones and inner portion of the mill. He put both his hands to work. [The left poured the grain into the mill, the right turned the millstone.] The grain which was ground by the rapid blows of the millstone poured out as flour. . . . At times he sang country songs and eased his labor with a rural tune. . . .

[After he had ground the grain, he mixed the flour with salt and water, formed the mixture into a round loaf, cut the impression of a cross on the top, and set the loaf to cook in the fireplace.]

While it baked, Simulus was not idle. He worked at another task, lest bread alone would not satisfy his hunger, and he prepared another dish to eat with the bread.

[Since he had no meat, he made a *moretum* of cheese, garlic, parsley, rue, coriander, salt, olive oil, and vinegar. All these ingredients were ground in a mortar with a pestle and carefully blended together.] . . .

Meanwhile, hard-working Scybale [Simulus's helper] plucked the bread out of the fireplace. Simulus happily took a piece in his hand. Now that he had put aside the fear of hunger and was free of anxiety, at least for this day, he tied leggings on his legs, covered his head with a leather cap, yoked his obedient oxen, drove them into the field, and sank his plow into the earth.

Moretum (anonymous), quoted in Jo-Ann Shelton, ed., *As The Romans Did: A Sourcebook in Roman Social History*. New York: Oxford University Press, 1988, pp. 162–63.

Document 5: Horatius, An Early Roman Military Hero

In times of danger, simple Roman farmers often became Roman soldiers charged with defending the state. And many stories were passed down through the centuries about the early military heroes who displayed unusual courage in the face of tremendous odds. Livy tells about one of the most famous such heroes, Horatius Cocles, who may or may not have been a real person. Shortly before the fall of the Monarchy (ca.509 B.C.), so the story goes, the Etruscans attempted to invade Rome via the only bridge leading to it over the Tiber. And brave Horatius single-handedly held back the enemy army while other Romans tore down the bridge behind him.

On the approach of the Etruscan army, the Romans abandoned their farmsteads and moved into the city. . . . The most vulnerable point [in the defenses] was the wooden bridge, and the Etruscans would have crossed it and forced an entrance into the city, had it not been for the courage of one man, Horatius Cocles—that great soldier whom the fortune of Rome gave to be her shield on that day of peril. . . . The enemy forces came pouring down the hill, while the Roman troops, throwing away their weapons, were behaving more like undisciplined rabble than a fighting force. Horatius acted promptly. . . . Urging [his comrades] . . . to destroy the bridge by fire or steel or any means they could muster, he offered to hold up the Etruscan advance . . . alone. Proudly he took his stand at the outer edge of the bridge. . . . The advancing enemy paused in sheer astonishment at such reckless courage. . . . With defiance in his eyes Horatius confronted the [enemy], challenging one after the other to single combat. . . . For a while they hung back, each waiting for his neighbor to make the first move until shame . . . drove them to action, and with a fierce cry they hurled their spears at the solitary figure who barred their way. Horatius caught the missiles on his shield and, resolute as ever, straddled the bridge and held his ground. The Etruscans moved forward . . . but their advance was suddenly checked by the crash of the falling bridge. . . . [They] could only stare in bewilderment as Horatius . . . plunged fully armed into the water and swam, through the missiles which fell thick around him, safely to the other side, where his friends were waiting to receive him.

Livy, *The History of Rome from Its Foundation*. Books 1–5 published as *Livy: The Early History of Rome*. Trans. Aubrey de Sélincourt. New York: Penguin Books, 1971, pp. 115–16.

Document 6: The Extensive Powers of Rome's Senate

Under the Republic, established shortly after the fall of the Monarchy about 509 B.C., the Roman people enjoyed a measurable degree of participation in their government, mainly through the open election of magistrates (public officials). However, the lion's share of power in republican Rome lay in the Senate, whose members were aristocrats who served for life. This sober and informative summary of that body's authority and powers, as it had evolved by the second century B.C., is by the Greek historian Polybius, an admirer of the Roman system.

The Senate, first of all, has control of the public treasury; for it controls almost every income and expenditure. With the exception of payments made to the consuls, the quaestors [state financial officers] are not allowed to make any payments for any necessary items or services without a decree of the Senate. And the expenditure which is by far heavier and of greater importance than any other, I mean the amount which the censors use every five years for the repair and construction of public works, this expenditure is regulated by the Senate, and a disbursement of funds is made to the censors by the Senate. Any crimes which have been committed in Italy and which require a public investigation, such as treason, conspiracy, poisoning, and murder, are the concern of the Senate.

In addition, if any private individual or any town in Italy needs arbitration or censure or help or protection, all these matters are the concern of the Senate. And if it is necessary to send an embassy to any country outside of Italy, in order to resolve a dispute, or to make a demand, or to give an order, or to receive submission, or to declare war, the Senate makes this task its concern. Similarly, when embassies arrive in Rome, everything—how it is necessary to treat them and what answer they should be given—is in the hands of the Senate. All in all, none of the matters mentioned above is controlled by the "people." And therefore, again, if someone resided in Rome at a time when the consuls were absent, to him the constitution appears entirely aristocratic. And many Greeks and many kings are convinced of this, because the Senate handles almost all matters having to do with them.

Someone might therefore ask, and not unreasonably, what part and how much of a part is left for the "people" in this constitution, considering that the Senate has control over each of the items which I mentioned above and, most importantly, that the Senate handles every income and expenditure; and again considering that the consuls have absolute authority as generals over the preparations for war, and absolute power in the field. . . .

When the consul sets off with his army, endowed with the powers I mentioned above, he seems to have absolute authority to carry out the task set for him. However, he is dependent on the "people" and the Senate, and he is not able to bring his projects to a conclusion without them. It is clear that the army must continually receive supplies, but, without the good will of the Senate, neither grain, nor clothing, nor pay can be supplied to the army. And so the plans of the generals are never carried out if the Senate decides to be negligent and obstructive. The fulfillment or nonfulfillment of the general's long-range goals and objectives also lie with the Senate, for it has the power to supersede him, when his year of office has come to an end, or of making him proconsul and retaining him in command. And the Senate also has the power to heighten and amplify the successes of the generals, or on the other hand to obscure and minimize them. The public salutes, which the Romans call triumphs, in which the generals bring before the eyes of the citizens clear evidence of their achievements, cannot be properly organized, and sometimes cannot be held at all, unless the Senate agrees and allots the necessary funds.

Similarly, the "people" are dependent upon the Senate, and must aim to please it both in public and in private. The censors assign numerous contracts for the construction and repair of public works throughout all of Italy, so many, in fact, that one could not easily count them. There are in addition many contracts relating to the use of rivers, harbors, orchards, mines, and farmlands, in short everything that falls under Roman sovereignty. Now it happens, of course, that all the work which the above-mentioned contracts entail is carried out by the masses, and almost everyone is involved in these contracts and the work they entail. Some men do the buying of the contract from the censors; other men are their partners; still others stand surety for the buyers; and some offer their own money to the state for these purposes. But it is the Senate which has control over all the matters just mentioned. The Senate can grant extensions of time; if an accident occurs, it can ease the requirements of the contract; and if the project turns out to be totally impossible, it can cancel the contract. And there are many different ways in which the Senate can greatly harm or greatly help those who deal with public revenues. To it, for example, are referred all the matters mentioned above. And, most importantly, from it are selected jurymen for most legal suits, of both public and private nature, especially where the charges are very serious. Therefore, because everyone is put at the mercy of the Senate and is fearful and uncertain about how it may act, they are cautious about obstructing and resisting its decisions.

Polybius, *Histories*, excerpted in Jo-Ann Shelton, ed., *As The Romans Did: A Sourcebook in Roman Social History*. New York: Oxford University Press, 1988, pp. 226–28.

Document 7: An Early Roman Treaty

In its early years, as it expanded outward and defeated its neighbors, Rome made treaties with these peoples, making them "allies" who were supposedly on more or less equal footing with the Romans. In reality, such equality was exaggerated, for an ally was expected to do Rome's bidding in most matters. In this excerpt from his history of Rome, the first-century-B.C. Greek writer Dionysius of Halicarnassus quotes from a treaty made between the Romans and the Latin League (an alliance of Latin cities that Rome had recently defeated) circa 493 B.C. The original document is now lost, but it or a copy of it may still have existed in his day.

At the same time a new treaty of peace and friendship was made with all the Latin cities and confirmed by oaths, inasmuch as they . . . were deemed to have lent ready assistance in the war against those who had seceded. ["Those" refers to the Aequi, Sabines, Volsci, and other non-Latin peoples in the region, who often fought the Romans and Latins.] The provisions of the treaty were as follows:

"Let there be peace between the Romans and all the Latin cities as long as heaven and earth shall stay in the same position. Let them neither make war upon one another themselves nor call in foreign enemies, nor grant safe passage to those who shall make war upon either, but let them assist one another with all their might when warred upon, and let each have an equal share of the spoils and booty taken in their common wars. Let suits relating to private contracts be judged within ten days and among the people where the contract was made. And let it not be permitted to add anything to, or take anything away from, this treaty except by the consent of both the Romans and all the Latins."

This was the treaty entered into by the Romans and the Latins with each other, and confirmed by their oaths sworn over sacrificial victims.

Dionysius of Halicarnassus, *Roman Antiquities,* quoted in Naphtali Lewis and Meyer Reinhold, eds., *Roman Civilization, Sourcebook I: The Republic.* New York: Harper and Row, 1966, p. 85.

Document 8: The State Guided by Fate and Prophecy

The early Romans were very religious, as well as superstitious. They not only believed in and regularly worshiped multiple gods, but also put great store in fate and prophecies of the future. In the fifth century B.C., they developed the custom of consulting the Sibylline Books (or "Books of Fate") either in times of crisis or to help make important state decisions. These books were collections of oracles (messages supposedly transmitted to humans from the gods) given by the Sibyl, a priestess at Cumae, in southwestern Italy. The Romans believed that careful interpretation of the oracles could reveal the correct action to be taken or policy to be enforced. As explained in this description of the books by Dionysius of Halicarnassus, the precious items were guarded and consulted by a special group of state priests.

Since the expulsion of the kings, the commonwealth, taking upon itself the guarding of these oracles, entrusts the care of them to persons of great distinction, who hold this office for life, being exempt from military service and from all civil employment, and it assigns public slaves to assist them, in whose absence the others are not permitted to inspect the oracles. In short, there is no possession of the Romans, sacred or profane, which they guard so carefully as they do the Sibylline oracles. They consult them, by order of the senate, when the state is in the grip of party strife or some great misfortune has happened to them in war, or some important prodigies or apparitions have been seen which are difficult of interpretation, as has often happened. These oracles till the time of the Marsian War, as it is called, were kept underground in a chest under the guard of ten men. But when the temple was burned after the close of the 173d Olympiad—either purposely, as some think, or by accident—these oracles together with all the offerings consecrated to the god were destroyed by the fire. Those which are now extant were scraped together from many places, some from the cities of Italy, others from Erythrae in Asia (whither three envoys were sent by vote of the senate to copy them), and others were brought from other cities, transcribed by private persons.

Dionysius of Halicarnassus, *Roman Antiquities*, quoted in Naphtali Lewis and Meyer Reinhold, eds., *Roman Civilization, Sourcebook I: The Republic*. New York: Harper and Row, 1966, p. 141.

Document 9: A Tradition of Borrowing from Others

The early Romans were not only hard-working, militarily aggressive, and very religious, they were also highly adaptive and opportunistic. Whenever they deemed it fit, which was often, they borrowed customs, ideas, and other aspects of foreign peoples, among the most important of these being the Etruscans, Samnites, and Greeks. The first-century-B.C. Roman historian Sallust explained this tendency of his ancestors in a tract describing a meeting of the Senate in which there was a debate about whether to execute some traitors without benefit of a trial. (He attributed the speech to Julius Caesar, but the words are more likely those of the historian himself.)

Our ancestors . . . never lacked wisdom or courage, and they were never too proud to take over a sound institution from another country. They borrowed most of their armour and weapons from the Samnites, and most of their magisterial insignia from the Etruscans. In short, if they thought anything that an ally or an enemy had was likely to suit them, they enthusiastically adopted it at Rome; for they would rather copy a good thing than be consumed with envy because they had not got it. In this period of imitation they followed the Greek custom of flogging citizens and executing convicted criminals. However, with the growth of the state, and the development of party strife resulting from the increase of population, innocent people were victimized, and other similar abuses grew up. To check them, the Porcian law was enacted, and other laws which allowed condemned persons the alternative of going into exile. This seems to me, gentlemen, a particularly strong argument against our making any innovation. For I cannot but think that there was greater virtue and wisdom in our predecessors, who with such small resources created such a vast empire, than there is in us, who find it as much as we can do to keep what they so nobly won.

Sallust, *The Jugurthine War/The Conspiracy of Catiline*. Trans. S.A. Handford. New York: Penguin Books, 1988, p. 220.

Document 10: Cincinnatus, Model for an Ideal Leader

Some of Rome's success in its rise to dominance in Italy and beyond can be attributed to the fact that most Romans believed in the moral rightness of their system. And one way the government reinforced and perpetuated this concept was to promote the memory of exceptional leaders, such as Lucius Quinctius Cincinnatus, a semi-legendary hero of the early Republic. Supposedly, he accepted the office of dictator in 458 B.C. to deal with a threat posed by the Aequi, a neighboring Italian tribe. A dictator was entitled to and usually did serve for six months during a national emergency and then stepped down. By contrast, having defeated the enemy army, Cincinnatus dutifully resigned his office after only sixteen days and returned to his farm. For this, he became a model for the ideal Roman leader, a man with old-fashioned values such as simplicity, selflessness, and patriotism, who risked his life for the state and sought no glory or personal power. Though in the years that followed most of Rome's leaders did not live up to this ideal, Cincinnatus remained a symbol of republican virtue, much as George Washington did (and still does) for most Americans.

Now I would solicit the particular attention of those numerous people who imagine that money is everything in this world, and that rank and ability are inseparable from wealth: let them observe that Cincinnatus, the one man in whom Rome reposed all her hope of survival, was at that moment working a little three-acre farm (now known as the Quinctian meadows) west of the Tiber, just opposite the spot where the shipyards are today. A mission from the city found him at work on his land—digging a ditch, maybe, or ploughing. Greetings were exchanged, and he was asked—with a prayer for God's blessing on himself and his country—to put on his toga and hear the Senate's instructions. This naturally surprised him, and, asking if all were well, he told his wife Racilia to run to their cottage and fetch his toga. The toga was brought, and wiping the grimy sweat from his hands and face he put it on; at once the envoys from the city saluted him, with congratulations, as Dictator, invited him to enter Rome, and informed him of the terrible danger of Minucius's army. A state vessel was waiting for him on the river, and on the city bank he was welcomed by his three sons who had come to meet him, then by other kinsmen and friends, and finally by nearly the whole body of senators. Closely attended by all these people and preceded by his lictors [attendants who carried symbols of Roman power] he was then escorted to his residence through streets lined with great crowds of common folk who, be it said, were by no means so pleased to see the new Dictator, as they thought his power excessive and dreaded the way in which he was likely to use it. . . .

[Cincinnatus quickly defeated the Aequi, then headed back to Rome, where] the Senate was convened by Quintus Fabius the City Prefect, and a decree was passed inviting Cincinnatus to enter in triumph with his troops. The chariot he rode in was preceded by the enemy commanders and the military standards, and followed by his army loaded with its spoils. We read in accounts of this great day that there was not a house in Rome but had a table spread with food before its door, for the entertainment of the soldiers who regaled themselves as they followed the triumphal chariot, singing and joking as befitted the occasion, like men out to enjoy themselves. . . .

Only the impending trial of Volscius [a former soldier] for perjury prevented Cincinnatus from resigning immediately. The tribunes who were thoroughly in awe of him made no attempt to interfere with the proceedings, and Volscius was found guilty and went into exile at Lanuvium. Cincinnatus finally resigned after holding office for fifteen days, having originally accepted it for a period of six months.

Livy, *The History of Rome from Its Foundation*. Books 1–5 published as *Livy: The Early History of Rome*. Trans. Aubrey de Sélincourt. New York: Penguin Books, 1971, pp. 213, 216.

Document 11: A Veteran Soldier Recalls His Years of Service

The Roman army was obviously one of the principal keys to Rome's success. For a long time it was composed mainly of landowners or other propertied men who served in a campaign when needed and then went back to civilian life until called up again, if ever. In the last republican centuries, however, with Roman armies fighting far from Italy and some campaigns lasting months or even years, some men signed on repeatedly for tours of duty, foreshadowing the advent of true career soldiers. Prominent among these men were highly respected low-ranking officers called centurions, each of whom commanded a century (at first 100 and later 80 men). In this excerpt from Livy's history of Rome, one such veteran centurion proudly recalls his service record.

Fellow citizens: I, Spurius Ligustinus, am descended from the Sabines. My father left me an acre of farmland and a small cottage, in which I was born and raised. And I live there even today. As soon as I reached manhood, my father married me to his brother's daughter, who brought with her nothing except her free birth and chastity and, with these, her fertility which would have filled even a wealthy home. We have six sons and two daughters, both of whom are now married. Four of our sons wear the *toga virilis* [garment of manhood], two still wear the *toga praetexta* [garment of boyhood].

I became a soldier in the consulship of Publius Sulpicius and Gaius Aurelius [i.e., 200 B.C.]. In the army which was taken to Macedonia to fight King Philip, I spent two years as a private. In the third year, because of my valor, Titus Quinctius Flamininus put me in charge of the tenth maniple of *hastati* [young men who fought in the first line of infantry]. After Philip and the Macedonians had been defeated, when we were brought back to Italy and discharged, I immediately set out for Spain as a volunteer soldier with the consul Marcus Porcius Cato. Those of you who served under him and under other generals, too, in a long army career, know that no one of all the generals now alive was a more perceptive observer and judge of valor. This general judged me worthy of commanding the first maniple of *hastati*. I became a volunteer soldier again for the third time in the army which was sent against King Antiochus and the Aetolians. Manius Acilius made me first centurion of the first century. When King Antiochus had been driven back and the Aetolians beaten, we were brought back to Italy. Two more times after that I served in campaigns where the legions were on duty for a year. Then I campaigned twice in Spain, once when Quintus Fulvius Flaccus was praetor and again when Tiberius Sempronius Gracchus was praetor. I was brought back from the province of Spain by Flaccus to appear with him in his triumph, along with others whom he brought back because of their valor. Asked by Tiberius Gracchus to return to the province, I returned. Four times within a few years I was chief centurion of the *triarii* [older, more experienced soldiers who made up the reserve, back-up line of infantry]. Thirty-four times I was rewarded by my generals for valor. I have received six Civic Crowns [the award for saving a Roman citizen's life]. I have served twenty-two years in the army, and I am over fifty years old. . . . But as long as anyone who is enrolling armies considers me a suitable soldier, I will never try to be excused from service. It is the prerogative of the military tribunes to judge me worthy of a rank, whatever that may be. I, for my part, will take care that no one in the army surpasses me in valor. That I have always done so, both my generals and those soldiers who served with me are my witnesses.

Livy, *The History of Rome from Its Foundation*, quoted in Jo-Ann Shelton, ed., *As The Romans Did: A Sourcebook in Roman Social History*. New York: Oxford University Press, 1988, pp. 256–57.

Document 12: Hannibal Crosses the Alps

The Second Punic War (218–201 B.C.) proved to be a tremendous test for the Roman army, as well as the Roman people as a whole, for at times Carthage, led by the brilliant and resourceful Hannibal, seemed on the brink of totally defeating Rome. Hannibal gained the initial upper hand when he surprised his opponents by taking an army over the Alps and into northern Italy, a feat that was before this assumed to be physically impossible. This graphic depiction of the treacherous crossing, including the Carthaginians' struggles against cold, ice, snow, steep slopes, and angry native tribesmen, is from Livy's great Roman history.

At the head of the column were the cavalry and elephants; Hannibal himself, with the pick of the infantry, brought up the rear, keeping his eyes open and alert for every contingency. Before long the column found itself on a narrowing track, one side of which was overhung by a precipitous wall of rock, and it was suddenly attacked. The natives, springing from their places of concealment, fiercely assaulted front and rear, leaping into the fray, hurling missiles, rolling down rocks from the heights above. The worst pressure was on Hannibal's rear; to meet it, his infantry faced-about—and it was clear enough that, had not the rear of the column been adequately protected, the Carthaginian losses would have been appalling. Even as it was the moment was critical, and disaster only just averted; for Hannibal hesitated to send his own division into the pass—to do so would have deprived the infantry of such support as he was himself providing for the cavalry—and his hesitation enabled the tribesmen to deliver a flank attack, cut the whole column in two, and establish themselves on the track. As a result, Hannibal, for one night, found himself cut off from his cavalry and baggage-train. Next day, however, as enemy activity weakened, a junction was effected between the two halves of the column and the defile was successfully passed, though not without losses, especially amongst the pack-animals.

Thenceforward there was no concerted opposition, the natives confining themselves to mere raids, in small parties, on front or rear, as the nature of the ground dictated, or as groups of stragglers, left behind or pressing on ahead of the column as the case might be, offered a tempting prey. The elephants proved both a blessing and a curse: for though getting them along the narrow and precipitous tracks caused serious delay, they were none the less a protection to the troops, as the natives, never having seen such creatures before, were afraid to come near them.

On the ninth day the army reached the summit [of a 10,000-foot-high mountain]. Most of the climb had been over trackless mountain-sides; frequently a wrong route was taken—sometimes through the deliberate deception of the guides, or, again, when some likely-looking valley would be entered by guess-work, without knowledge of whither it led. There was a two days' halt on the summit, to rest the men after the exhausting climb and the fighting. Some of the pack-animals which had fallen amongst the rocks managed, by following the army's tracks, to find their way into camp. The troops had indeed endured hardships enough; but there was worse to come. It was the season of the setting of the Pleiades [i.e., late October]. Winter was near—and it began to snow. Getting on the move at dawn, the army struggled slowly forward over snow-covered ground, the hopelessness of utter exhaustion in every face. Seeing their despair, Hannibal rode ahead and at a point of vantage which afforded a prospect of a vast extent of country, he gave the order to halt, pointing to Italy far below, and the Po Valley beyond the foothills of the Alps. 'My men,' he said, 'you are at this moment passing the protective barrier of Italy—nay more, you are walking over the very walls of Rome. Henceforward all will be easy going—no more hills to climb. After a fight or two you will have the capital of Italy, the citadel of Rome, in the hollow of your hands.'

The march continued, more or less without molestation from the natives, who confined themselves to petty raids when they saw a chance of stealing something. Unfortunately, however, as in most parts of the Alps the descent on the Italian side, being shorter, is correspondingly steeper, the going was much more difficult than it had been during the ascent. The track was almost everywhere precipitous, narrow, and slippery; it was impossible for a man to keep his feet; the least stumble meant a fall, and a fall a slide, so that there was indescribable confusion, men and beasts stumbling and slipping on top of each other.

Soon, they found themselves on the edge of a precipice—a narrow cliff falling away so sheer that even a lightly-armed soldier could hardly have got down it by feeling his way and clinging to such bushes and stumps as presented themselves. It must always have been a most awkward spot, but a recent landslide had converted it on this occasion to a perpendicular drop of nearly a thousand feet. On the brink the cavalry drew rein—their journey seemed to be over. Hannibal, in the rear, did not yet know what had brought the column to a halt; but when the message was passed to him that there was no possibility of proceeding, he went in person to reconnoitre. It was clear to him that a detour would have to be made, however long it might prove to be, over the trackless and untrodden slopes in the vicinity. But even so he was no luckier; progress was impossible, for though there was good foothold in the quite shallow layer of soft fresh snow which had covered the old snow underneath, nevertheless as soon as it had been trampled and dispersed by the feet of all those men and animals, there was left to tread upon only the bare ice and liquid slush of melting snow underneath. The result was a horrible struggle, the ice affording no foothold in any case, and least of all on a steep slope; when a man tried by hands or knees to get on his feet again, even those useless supports slipped from under him and let him down; there were no stumps or roots anywhere to afford a purchase to either foot or hand; in short, there was nothing for it but to roll and slither on the smooth ice and melting snow. Sometimes the mules' weight would drive their hoofs through into the lower layer of old snow; they would fall and, once down, lashing savagely out in their struggles to rise, they would break right through it, so that as often as not they were held as in a vice by a thick layer of hard ice.

When it became apparent that both men and beasts were wearing themselves out to no purpose, a space was cleared—with the greatest labour because of the amount of snow to be dug and carted away—and camp was pitched, high up on the ridge. The next task was to construct some sort of passable track down the precipice, for by no other route could the army proceed. It was necessary to cut through rock, a problem they solved by the ingenious application of heat and moisture; large trees were felled and lopped, and a huge pile of timber erected; this, with the opportune help of a strong wind, was set on fire, and when the rock was sufficiently heated the men's rations of sour wine were flung upon it, to render it friable. They then got to work with picks on the heated rock, and opened a sort of zigzag track, to minimize the steepness of the descent, and were able, in consequence, to get the pack animals, and even the elephants, down it.

Four days were spent in the neighbourhood of this precipice; the animals came near to dying of starvation, for on most of the peaks nothing grows, or, if there is any pasture, the snow covers it. Lower down there are sunny hills and valleys and woods with streams flowing by: country, in fact, more worthy for men to dwell in. There the beasts were put out to pasture, and the troops given three days' rest to recover from the fatigue of their road-building.

Thence the descent was continued to the plains—a kindlier region, with kindlier inhabitants.

Livy, *The History of Rome from Its Foundation.* Books 21–30 published as *Livy: The War With Hannibal.* Trans. Aubrey de Sélincourt. New York: Penguin, 1972, pp. 59–62.

Document 13: The Romans Slow Hannibal Down with Delaying Tactics

In dealing with enemies, the Romans had long been successful in the application of brute force in an ordered, skilled way. But at first, this approach did not work with Hannibal, who, after entering Italy, defeated one Roman army after another. Then Fabius Maximus was appointed dictator. He adopted the novel and wiser approach of purposely avoiding large-scale battle with Hannibal, choosing instead to wear the enemy down by constantly following him at a safe distance and harassing his food foragers and baggage train. This synopsis of these tactics, known as "Fabian" ever since, comes from the first-century-A.D. Greek writer Plutarch's biography of Fabius. As Plutarch reports, the dictator's unusual tactics did not sit well initially with his countrymen, who had to sit idly by and watch the Carthaginians ravage the Italian countryside.

By encouraging the people in this way to fix their thoughts upon religious matters, Fabius contrived to strengthen their confidence in the future. For his part, however, he trusted entirely to his own efforts to win the victory, since he believed that the gods grant men success according to the courage and wisdom that they display, and in this frame of mind he turned his attention to Hannibal. He was determined not to fight a pitched battle, and since he had time and manpower and money on his side, his plan was to exhaust his opponent's strength, which was now at its peak, by means of delaying tactics, and gradually to wear down his small army and meagre resources. With this object in view he always bivouacked [set up temporary camps] in mountainous country, where he was out of reach of the enemy's cavalry, and at the same time hung menacingly over the Carthaginian camp. If the enemy stayed still, he did the same. If they moved, he would make a detour, descend a little distance from the heights, and show himself just far enough away to prevent himself from being forced into an action against his will, but near enough to create the suspicion from the very slowness of his movements that he might be about to attack. But the Romans soon became contemptuous of these time-killing tactics and Fabius began to be despised in his own camp, while the enemy—with one exception—were convinced that he was a nonentity who was utterly devoid of warlike spirit. The exception was Hannibal. He, and he alone, perceived his opponent's shrewdness and divined the strategy which Fabius had laid down for the war. He therefore made up his mind that he must use every trick to lure or force the enemy into battle, or else the Carthaginian cause was lost, since his men were being prevented from exploiting their superiority in training, while their manpower and resources, in which they were inferior to the Romans, were being steadily exhausted to no purpose. And so he brought into play all the arts and stratagems of war and tried every one in turn, like a skilful wrestler, who watches for his opportunity to secure a hold on his adversary. First he would attack Fabius's army directly, then try to throw it into confusion, then draw him on from one place to another, all in the effort to lure him away from the safety of his defensive tactics. Fabius, however, had complete faith in his plan, followed it out consistently, and refused to be drawn. But he was provoked by his master of horse, Minucius, a headstrong officer who longed for action regardless of the circumstances, and who tried to increase his popularity by raising empty hopes and working up his men's spirits to a state of wild enthusiasm. The soldiers mocked at Fabius and contemptuously called him Hannibal's governess, but they thought Minucius a great man and a general worthy of Rome. This encouraged the master of horse to indulge his boastful arrogance more than ever and to make fun of Fabius's tactics of encamping on high ground, where, as he put it, the dictator took great trouble to provide them with splendid seats to witness the spectacle of Italy being laid waste with fire and sword. He was also fond of asking Fabius's friends whether he thought he was leading the troops up to heaven, since he had evidently ceased to take any interest in events on earth, or whether he was enveloping them in clouds and mist simply to escape from the enemy. Fabius's friends reported these remarks, and urged him to wipe out such aspersions on his courage by risking a battle. His answer was: 'In that case I should be an even greater coward than they say I am, if I were to abandon the plans I believe to be right because of a few sneers and words of abuse. There is nothing shameful in experiencing fear for your country's sake.'

Plutarch, *Life of Fabius*, in *Makers of Rome: Nine Lives By Plutarch*. Trans. Ian Scott-Kilvert. New York: Penguin Books, 1965, pp. 58–59.

Document 14: Hannibal and Scipio: A Meeting of Giants

In 202 B.C., on the eve of the climax of the Second Punic War, a fateful meeting took place on the plain of Zama, near Carthage. For the first time, Hannibal came face to face with his chief rival, Publius Cornelius Scipio

(Later called "Africanus"), whose army was camped only four miles from Hannibal's. This is Livy's account of the beginning of the meeting, which unfortunately did not end with a truce or other peace accord. A great battle ensued, Scipio won, and only then did Carthage sue for peace. (Note that Livy's inclusion of specific quotes by Hannibal should not be taken at face value. In most cases, the actual content of ancient battle speeches and meetings among commanders has been lost. In such cases, it was the accepted custom of ancient writers to "reconstruct" as best they could what they believed the characters were likely to have said under the circumstances.)

Scipio acceded to Hannibal's request for a conference, and the two generals agreed to advance the position of their respective camps so as to facilitate their meeting. Scipio established himself near Naraggara in a favourable position within javelin-range of water; Hannibal occupied a hill four miles away, safe and convenient enough except for its distance from water. Between the two positions a spot in full view from every side was chosen for the meeting, to ensure against a treacherous attack.

Exactly half-way between the opposing ranks of armed men, each attended by an interpreter, the generals met. They were not only the two greatest soldiers of their time, but the equals of any king or commander in the whole history of the world. For a minute mutual admiration struck them dumb, and they looked at each other in silence. Hannibal was the first to speak. 'If fate,' he said, 'has decreed that I who was the aggressor in the war with Rome, and so many times have had victory almost within my grasp, should of my own will come to ask for peace, I rejoice at least that destiny has given me you, and no other, from whom to ask it. You have many titles to honour, and amongst them, for you too, it will not be the least to have received the submission of Hannibal, to whom the gods gave victory over so many Roman generals, and to have brought to an end this war which was made memorable by your defeats before ever it was marked by ours. May it not also be a pretty example of the irony of fate that I took up arms when your father was consul, fought against him my first battle with a Roman general, and now come, unarmed, to his son to sue for peace? Assuredly it would have been best if the gods had given our fathers contentment with what was their own—you with ruling Italy, us with ruling Africa. Not even you can find Sicily and Sardinia adequate compensation for the loss of so many fleets and armies and the deaths of so many fine officers: but what is done is done—it may be censured, but it cannot be altered.'

Livy, *The History of Rome from Its Foundation.* Books 21–30 published as *Livy: The War With Hannibal.* Trans. Aubrey de Sélincourt. New York: Penguin, 1972, pp. 654–55.

Document 15: "Carthage Must Be Destroyed"

Cato the Elder (234–149 B.C.) was a conservative Roman senator who came, as many Romans did, to hate Carthage because of the trouble and grief it had caused Rome over the years. And though the two nations remained at peace for decades following the Second Punic War, Cato became determined to eradicate what he viewed as an eternal enemy. By deftly using his considerable influence in the Senate, more than any other man Cato brought about Carthage's final destruction, as explained in this famous passage from Plutarch's biography of Cato.

Some people consider that the last of his political achievements was the destruction of Carthage. In the military sense it was the younger Scipio who brought this about, but the fact that the Romans went to war at all was very largely the consequence of Cato's advice. This was how it happened. Cato was sent out on a diplomatic mission to investigate the causes of a dispute between the Carthaginians and Masinissa the king of Numidia, who were at this time [150 B.C.] at war. Masinissa had been a friend of the Roman people from the first, whereas the Carthaginians had entered into treaty relations with Rome only after the defeat which they had suffered at the hands of Scipio Africanus, and this settlement had stripped them of their empire and compelled them to pay a heavy tribute to Rome. Nevertheless it was at once apparent to Cato that the city was by no means crushed nor impoverished as the Romans imagined. He found it teeming with a new generation of fighting men, overflowing with wealth, amply stocked with weapons and military supplies of every kind, and full of confidence at this revival of its strength. He drew the conclusion that this was no time for the Romans to occupy themselves with regulating the affairs of Masinissa and the Numidians, but that unless they found means to crush a city which had always borne them an undying hatred and had now recovered its power to an incredible extent, they would find themselves as gravely threatened as before. He therefore returned with all speed to Rome, and warned the Senate that the overwhelming defeats and misfortunes which the Carthaginians had suffered had done much to diminish their recklessness and over-confidence, but little to impair their strength, and that they were likely to emerge not weaker but more experienced in war. He was convinced that this present dispute with the Numidians was merely the prelude to an attack upon Rome, and that the peace and the treaty which existed between them were a convenient fiction to cover a period of suspense, until a suitable moment should arrive to begin a war.

As he ended this speech it is said that Cato shook out the folds of his toga and contrived to drop some Libyan figs on the floor of the Senate-house, and when the senators admired their size and beauty he remarked that the country which produced them was only three days' sail from Rome. Afterwards he adopted a still more forceful method of driving home his point: whenever his opinion was called for on any subject, he invariably concluded with the words, 'And furthermore it is my opinion that Carthage must be destroyed!' On the other hand [another senator named] Publius Scipio Nasica made a point of adding the phrase, 'And in my view Carthage must be spared!' Scipio had already observed, no doubt, that the Roman people were by this time indulging in many excesses, and that the insolence occasioned by its prosperity prompted it to cast aside the control of the Senate and force the whole state to follow in whichever direction the impulses of the masses might lead. He was therefore in favour of keeping the fear of Carthage hanging over the people as a check upon their arrogance, and he evidently also believed that although Carthage was not strong enough to threaten the Romans, she was not so weak that they could afford to despise her. But this was precisely the danger that Cato feared, namely that at a time when the Romans were intoxicated and carried away by their new-found power, they should allow a city which had always been great and had now been sobered by calamity to continue to threaten them. He believed that it was best to free the Romans from any fear of outside danger, so that they could devote themselves wholeheartedly to reforming their own shortcomings and abuses at home.

This is the way in which Cato is said to have brought about the third and last war against Carthage. He died almost immediately after it had begun, leaving a prophecy that it would be ended by a man who was still young, but who had already as a military tribune given remarkable proofs of his intelligence and daring in his encounters with the enemy. [That man turned out to be Scipio Aemilianus, who ordered the final destruction of Carthage.]

Plutarch, *Life of Cato*, in *Makers of Rome: Nine Lives By Plutarch*. Trans. Ian Scott-Kilvert. New York: Penguin Books, 1965, pp. 149–50.

Document 16: Rome's Next Victim: Greece

Even while the Romans were fighting Carthage, astute politicians and thinkers in various corners of the Mediterranean world began to recognize that Rome probably would not stop with acquiring domination of the sea's western sphere. It seemed clear to these people that the Greek states in the eastern Mediterranean would inevitably become the next victims of Roman imperialism (a nation's drive to expand its power and influence at the expense of other nations and peoples). In 213 B.C., a Greek orator named Agelaus made this impassioned, moving, and, as it turned out, prophetic plea for the Greeks to present a united front against the rising Roman threat. Unfortunately for Greece, his words fell largely on deaf ears.

'It would be best if the Greeks never went to war with one another, if they could regard it as the greatest gift of the gods for them all to speak with one voice, and could join hands like men who are crossing a river; in this way they could unite to repulse the incursions of the barbarians and to preserve themselves and their cities. But if we have no hope of achieving such a degree of unity for the whole country, let me impress upon you how important it is at least for the present that we should consult one another and remain on our guard, in view of the huge armies which have been mobilized, and the vast scale of the war which is now being waged in the west. For it must already be obvious to all those who pay even the slightest attention to affairs of state that whether the Carthaginians defeat the Romans or the Romans the Carthaginians, the victors will by no means be satisfied with the sovereignty of Italy and Sicily, but will come here, and will advance both their forces and their ambitions beyond the bounds of justice. I therefore beg you all to be on your guard against this danger, and I appeal especially to King Philip. For you the safest policy, instead of wearing down the Greeks and making them an easy prey for the invader, is to take care of them as you would of your own body, and to protect every province of Greece as you would if it were a part of your own dominions. If you follow this policy, the Greeks will be your friends and your faithful allies in case of attack, and foreigners will be the less inclined to plot against your throne, because they will be discouraged by the loyalty of the Greeks towards you. But if you yearn for a field of action, then turn your attention to the west, keep it fixed on the wars in Italy, and bide your time, so that when the moment comes, you may enter the contest for the sovereignty of the whole world. Now the present moment is by no means unfavourable to such hopes. But you must, I entreat you, put aside your differences with the Greeks and your campaigns against them until times have become more settled, and concern yourself first and foremost with this aspect of the situation which I have just mentioned, so that you retain the power to make peace or war with them as you think best. For if you wait until the clouds which are now gathering in the west settle upon Greece, I very much fear that these truces and wars and games at which we now play may have been knocked out of our hands so completely that we shall be praying to the gods to grant us still this power of fighting or making peace with one another as we choose, in other words of being left the capacity to settle our own disputes.'

Quoted in Polybius, *Histories*, published as *Polybius: The Rise of the Roman Empire*. Trans. Ian Scott-Kilvert. New York: Penguin Books, 1979, pp. 299–300.

Document 17: Why Rome's Military Was Superior to That of the Greeks

Two principal factors made Rome's conquest of the Greek lands possible, the first being a glaring lack of unity among these kingdoms and city-states. Second, the Roman military system ultimately proved superior to the Greek one. In this excerpt from his history of Rome, Polybius discusses the strengths of the core element of the Greek system—the Macedonian phalanx—but he also points out its fatal weaknesses. He then goes on to explain why Roman battle formations are more flexible and efficient.

In the past the Macedonian formation was proved by operational experience to be superior to the others which were in use in Asia and Greece, while the Roman system overcame those employed in Africa and among all the peoples of Western Europe. In our own times we have seen both the two formations and the soldiers of the two nations matched against one another, not just once but on many occasions. It should prove a useful exercise, and one well worth the trouble, to study the differences between them, and to discover the reason why on the battlefield the Romans have always proved the victors and carried off the prize. If we examine the matter in this way we shall not, like the ignorant majority of mankind, speak merely in terms of chance, and congratulate the victors without giving the reasons, but shall be able to pay them the praise and admiration they deserve because we have come to understand the causes of their success. . . .

There are a number of factors which make it easy to understand that so long as the phalanx retains its characteristic form and strength nothing can withstand its charge or resist it face to face. When the phalanx is closed up for action, each man with his arms occupies a space of three feet. The pike he carries was earlier designed to be twenty-four feet long, but as adapted to current practice was shortened to twenty-one, and from this we must subtract the space between the bearer's hands and the rear portion of the pike which keeps it balanced and couched. This amounts to six feet in all, from which it is clear that the pike will project fifteen feet in front of the body of each hoplite when he advances against the enemy grasping it with both hands. This also means that while the pikes of the men in the second, third, and fourth ranks naturally extend further than those of the fifth rank, yet even the latter will still project three feet in front of the men in the first rank. I am assuming of course that the phalanx keeps its characteristic order, and is closed up both from the rear and on the flanks. . . .

At any rate if my description is true and exact, it follows that each man in the front rank will have the points of five pikes extending in front of him, each point being three feet ahead of the one behind.

From these facts we can easily picture the nature and the tremendous power of a charge by the whole phalanx, when it advances sixteen deep with levelled pikes. Of these sixteen ranks those who are stationed further back than the fifth cannot use their pikes to take an active part in the battle. They therefore do not level them man against man, but hold them with the points tilted upwards over the shoulders of the men in front. In this way they give protection to the whole phalanx from above, for the pikes are massed so closely that they can keep off any missiles which might clear the heads of the front ranks and strike those immediately behind them. Once the charge is launched, these rear ranks by the sheer pressure of their bodily weight greatly increase its momentum and make it impossible for the foremost ranks to face about.

I have described both in general terms and in detail the composition of the phalanx. I must now for purposes of comparison explain the special features of Roman equipment and tactical formation, and the differences which distinguish the two. With the Romans each soldier in full armour also occupies a space three feet wide. However, according to the Roman methods of fighting each man makes his movements individually: not only does he defend his body with his long shield, constantly moving it to meet a threatened blow, but he uses his sword both for cutting and for thrusting. Obviously these tactics require a more open order and an interval between the men, and in practice each soldier needs to be at least three feet from those in the same rank and from those in front of and behind him if he is to perform his function efficiently. The result of these dispositions is that each Roman soldier has to face two men in the front rank of the phalanx, and so has to encounter and fight against ten spear points. It is impossible for one man to cut through all of these once the battle lines are engaged, nor is it easy to force the points away; moreover, in the Roman formation the rear ranks do not support the front, either in forcing the spears away or in the use of their swords. It is easy to understand then, as I mentioned at the beginning, how nothing can withstand the frontal assault of the phalanx so long as it retains its characteristic formation and strength.

What then is the factor which enables the Romans to win the battle and causes those who use the phalanx to fail? The answer is that in war the times and places for action are unlimited, whereas the phalanx requires one time and one type of ground only in order to produce its peculiar effect. Now if the enemy were compelled to position themselves according to the times and places demanded by the phalanx whenever an important battle was imminent, no doubt those who employ the phalanx would always carry off the victory for the reasons I have given above. But if it is quite possible, even easy, to evade its irresistible charge, how can the phalanx any longer be considered formidable? Again, it is generally admitted that its use requires flat and level ground which is unencumbered by any obstacles such as ditches, gullies, depressions, ridges and watercourses, all of which are sufficient to hinder and dislocate such a formation. There is general agreement that it is almost impossible, or at any rate exceedingly rare, to find a stretch of country of say two or three miles or more which contains no obstacles of this kind. But even assuming that such an arena could be found, if the enemy refuses to come down into it, but prefers to traverse the country sacking the towns and devastating the territories of our allies, what purpose can the phalanx serve? If it remains on the ground which suits it best, not only is it unable to assist its allies, but it cannot even ensure its own safety, for the transport of its supplies will easily be stopped by the enemy when they have undisputed command of the open country. On the other hand, if it leaves the terrain which favours it and attempts an action elsewhere, it will easily be defeated. Or again, supposing that the enemy does decide to descend into the plain and fight there, but, instead of committing his entire force to the battle when the phalanx has its one opportunity to charge, keeps even a small part of it in reserve at the moment when the main action takes place, it is easy to forecast what will happen from the tactics which the Romans are now putting into practice.

The outcome indeed does not need to be demonstrated by argument: we need only refer to accomplished facts. The Romans do not attempt to make their line numerically equal to the enemy's, nor do they expose the whole strength of the legions to a frontal attack by the phalanx. Instead they keep part of the forces in reserve while the rest engage the enemy. Later in the battle, whether the phalanx in its charge drives back the troops opposed to it or is driven back by them, in either event it loses its own peculiar formation. For either in pursuing a retreating enemy or falling back before an oncoming one, the phalanx leaves behind the other units of its own army; at this point the enemy's reserves can occupy the space the phalanx has vacated, and are no longer obliged to attack from the front, but can fall upon it from flank and rear. When it is thus easy to deny the phalanx the opportunities it needs and to minimize the advantages it enjoys, and also impossible to prevent the enemy from acting against it, does it not follow that the difference between these two systems is enormous?

Besides this, those who rely on the phalanx are obliged to march across and encamp on ground of every description; they must occupy favourable positions in advance, besiege others and be besieged themselves and deal with unexpected appearances of the enemy. All these eventualities are part and parcel of war, and may have an important or a decisive effect on the final victory. In all these situations the Macedonian formation is sometimes of little use, and sometimes of none at all, because the phalanx soldier cannot operate either in smaller units or singly, whereas the Roman formation is highly flexible. Every Roman soldier, once he is armed and goes into action, can adapt himself equally well to any place or time and meet an attack from any quarter. He is likewise equally well-prepared and needs to make no change whether he has to fight with the main body or with a detachment, in maniples or singly. Accordingly, since the effective use of the parts of the Roman army is so much superior, their plans are much more likely to achieve success than those of others. I have felt obliged to deal with this subject at some length, because so many Greeks on those occasions when the Macedonians suffered defeat regarded such an event as almost incredible, and many will still be at a loss to understand why and how the phalanx proves inferior by comparison with the Roman method of arming their troops.

Polybius, *Histories*, published as *Polybius: The Rise of the Roman Empire*. Trans. Ian Scott-Kilvert. New York: Penguin Books, 1979, pp. 508–73.

Document 18: Roman Absorption of Greek Culture

The following tract by the late, noted classical historian Chester G. Starr discusses several aspects of the pronounced cultural borrowing that accom-

panied the relationship between Rome and Greece. A clear double standard was at work here. On the one hand, in Roman eyes the Hellenistic Greeks (i.e., those living in the three-century-long historical age following the death of Alexander the Great in 323 B.C.) were not the Romans' political equals. On the other, the Greeks possessed a high culture that was undeniably superior to that of Rome. So the always practical Romans conquered Greece and freely adopted those Greek customs and ideas that met their needs or struck their fancy. The result was the Greco-Roman cultural mix that eventually came to be called "classical civilization." And in this way, the rise of Rome helped to bring about the perpetuation of Greece.

From its earliest days Rome had been deeply affected by Greek culture, either directly or via Etruscan intermediaries. In the early fifth century this tie had weakened in central Italy. The Romans lived within a narrow world, culturally speaking, during the period in which they built up their own system of government and conquered Italy. Rome thus had no direct contact with the great days of classic Greek culture; its ties were resumed only from the early third century onward. By this time Greek civilization had passed into its Hellenistic phase, more superficial but far more widely attractive. While the Romans needed no lessons in political or military skill from the east, they showed ever greater interest in its culture.

Roman armies and generals brought back much of the physical achievement of this world from southern Italy, Sicily, and the Hellenistic east. Marcellus, the conqueror of Syracuse, returned with cargoes of statues which he erected in public places to embellish Rome; Aemilius Paullus, who defeated Perseus [son of the Macedonian King Philip V], brought the Macedonian state library to Rome; Mummius sacked Corinth before destroying it.

Men, too, came in tremendous numbers; the Roman conquest of Epirus alone netted 150,000 slaves in 167. Many of these went to man Roman farms and ranches, but some men who were enslaved were cultured, like the comedian Terence (P. Terentius Afer, c. 195–59). [The Greek historian] Polybius and other Greek leaders were brought in 167 to Rome as hostages. Others, including the philosophic leaders of Athens in 155, came as ambassadors or were drawn by the increasing wealth and power of the new Mediterranean capital. The Romans themselves, who had no developed culture of their own, proved amazingly receptive to many aspects of Hellenistic civilization.

Much of what they took was on the level of entertainment or physical pleasure. The first barber came from Sicily to a Latin town in 300; professional cooks soon made their appearance in Rome.

Aristocrats began to build more luxurious mansions, equipped with the best of Hellenistic furniture and comforts; to improve their taste in one respect the poet Q. Ennius (239–169) composed a manual *On the Art of Pleasant Eating.* . . .

Hellenistic educational principles also came to Rome. To replace the archaic Twelve Tables, the earlier primer, Livius Andronicus translated the *Odyssey* into Latin; and Greek rhetoricians and grammarians began to be sought by noble families as tutors for their sons. Rhetoric [the art of persuasive oratory] thus was a principal vehicle by which Greek ideas spread in Rome. Grammarians ameliorated the roughness and the poverty in vocabulary of the Latin language and improved its fundamental qualities of conciseness, sonority, and logical directness. By 133 Latin had become a literary tongue, and its aristocratic speakers at least were at home in the artistic, literary, and intellectual heritage of the Hellenistic world.

During the first waves of Hellenistic influence through the third and second centuries the Romans appear almost entirely as borrowers from the riches of the east. Yet it would be incorrect to infer that Roman culture was thenceforth simply a branch of Hellenistic civilization, though this inference is often made by modern scholars. In reality ideas and motifs underwent a subtle, but significant change in their sea passage from east to west.

Down to the late second century Roman independence showed itself primarily in the refusal of the Romans to surrender completely to alien ways. The hardheaded Roman citizenry was quite willing to take over what it deemed useful, but it showed little interest in the abstract or theoretical achievements of Hellenistic civilization. In science the Romans were attracted principally by the practical manuals on agricultural management. . . .

[Roman] aristocrats were sufficiently self-conscious and open-minded to be ready to accept Greek ethical thinking as a basis for their lives. The Stoics, in particular, had a view of the universe as divinely ordered which appealed to the Romans especially after the great second-century Stoic Panaetius (*c.* 185–09) reformed his school's doctrines on the inevitability of a world conflagration and the hopeless imperfection of all men save the pitiless and perfect Wise Man. Stoic ethical and political theory, as taught by Panaetius at Rome, accorded well with the Roman sense of duty, though it also reinforced the growing individualism of the aristocrats. The more abstract ideas of Stoic logical and physical theory, however, gained little attention. In assessing the increasing polish of Roman aristocrats we must always remember that the cultured friend of Panaetius, Polybius, and Terence, the high-born Scipio Aemilianus, was also the leader of the Roman army in the ruthless destruction of Carthage.

In the arts and architecture too little survives for us to see clearly the process of Roman adaptation, though the remains of Pompeii suggest that this minor Italian town was shifting from Greek to Roman styles by the end of the second century; by this date Roman builders were using travertine limestone and also concrete, both of which were to permit bolder experiments in architecture. In literature, however, the course of events is clearer. Plautus and Terence both adapted Greek plots for Roman production, the former in more slapstick manner, the latter in more sophisticated delineation of character; yet their plays have an undoubted Roman spirit. They wrote, moreover, in Latin—of all peoples with whom the Greeks came into contact the Romans were the only ones to create an independent literary speech.

Before the end of the second century Roman authors and, increasingly, Roman thinkers and artists were to begin to show the fruits of the entry of Hellenistic civilization into Rome. The product was a synthesis of Greek forms and techniques and Roman spirit into what must be termed a Greco-Roman culture, or perhaps better, a general Mediterranean upper-class culture. The full fruits of this synthesis were to be attained only after the Romans and their subjects had both come to accept the responsibilities and the yoke of empire. That acceptance required a terrific upheaval and reorganization covering a full century and a half.

Chronology

B.C.

ca. 1200–ca. 900
Approximate period of Italy's Iron Age, in which people learned to fashion tools and weapons made of iron.

ca. 1000 (and probably before)
Latin tribesmen establish small villages on some of the seven hills marking the site of the future city of Rome.

753
Traditional founding date for the city of Rome by Romulus (as computed and accepted by Roman scholars some seven centuries later).

753–717
Supposed years of Romulus's reign as Rome's first king.

534–509
Supposed years that Tarquinius Superbus, Rome's last king, reigned.

509
The leading Roman landowners throw out their last king and establish the Roman Republic.

496
The Romans defeat the other members of the Latin League at Lake Regillus.

ca. 451–450
The Twelve Tables, Rome's first law code, are inscribed and set up.

396
After a long siege, the Romans capture the important Etruscan town of Veii.

390
At the Allia River, a Roman army suffers a major defeat at the hands of a force of invading Gauls, who proceed to sack Rome.

340–338
Rome defeats the Latin League, dissolves it, and incorporates the territories of some of its members into the growing Roman state.

312
Construction of Rome's first major road, the Appian Way, and its first aqueduct, the Aqua Appia, begins.

ca. 289
Rome mints its first coins.

280–275
The Romans fight several battles with the Greek Hellenistic king Pyrrhus, who has come to the aid of the Greek cities of southern Italy; his victories are so costly that he eventually abandons the Italian Greeks to their fate.

265
Having gained control of the Italian Greek cities, Rome is master of the whole Italian peninsula.

264–241
The First Punic War, in which Rome defeats the maritime empire of Carthage.

218–201
Rome fights Carthage again in the Second Punic War, in which the Carthaginian general Hannibal crosses the Alps, invades Italy, and delivers the Romans one crippling defeat after another.

216
Hannibal crushes a large Roman army at Cannae (in southeastern Italy); Roman casualties exceed fifty thousand.

202
After the Romans weather the storm and rebound, their greatest general, Scipio Africanus, defeats Hannibal on the plain of Zama (in North Africa).

200–197
The Romans defeat Macedonia in the Second Macedonian War.

190
A Roman army defeats the Seleucid king, Antiochus III, at Magnesia (in Asia Minor).

168
The Third Macedonian War comes to a close as the Romans defeat Macedonia's King Perseus; the Macedonian kingdom is dismantled.

149–146
Rome annihilates Carthage in the Third Punic War.

146
The Romans destroy the Greek city of Corinth as an object lesson to other Greeks who might consider opposing Rome; most of the Mediterranean world is now under Roman domination.

For Further Research

Ancient Sources Relating to Rome's Rise

Paul J. Alexander, ed., *The Ancient World: To 300 A.D.* New York: Macmillan, 1963.

Appian, *Roman History*. Trans. Horace White. Cambridge, MA: Harvard University Press, 1964; also excerpted in *Appian: The Civil Wars*. Trans. John Carter. New York: Penguin Books, 1996.

Diodorus Siculus, *Library of History*. Vol. 3. Trans. C.H. Oldfather. Cambridge, MA: Harvard University Press, 1961.

Dionysius of Halicarnassus, *Roman Antiquities*. 7 vols. Trans. Earnest Cary. Cambridge, MA: Harvard University Press, 1963.

Bernard Knox, ed., *The Norton Book of Classical Literature*. New York: W.W. Norton, 1993.

Naphtali Lewis and Meyer Reinhold, eds., *Roman Civilization, Sourcebook 1: The Republic*. New York: Harper and Row, 1966.

Livy, *The History of Rome from Its Foundation*. Books 1–5 published as *Livy: The Early History of Rome*. Trans. Aubrey de Sélincourt. New York: Penguin Books, 1971; and books 21–30 published as *Livy: The War with Hannibal*. Trans. Aubrey de Sélincourt. New York: Penguin Books, 1972.

Plutarch, *Parallel Lives*, published complete as *Lives of the Noble Grecians and Romans*. Trans. John Dryden. New York: Random House, 1932; also excerpted in *Fall of the Roman Republic: Six Lives by Plutarch*. Trans. Rex Warner. New York: Penguin Books, 1972; and *Makers of Rome: Nine Lives by Plutarch*. Trans. Ian Scott-Kilvert. New York: Penguin Books, 1965.

Polybius, *The Histories*, published as *Polybius: The Rise of the Roman Empire*. Trans. Ian Scott-Kilvert. New York: Penguin Books, 1979.

Sallust, *The Jugurthine War/The Conspiracy of Catiline*. Trans. S.A. Handford. New York: Penguin Books, 1988.

Jo-Ann Shelton, ed., *As the Romans Did: A Sourcebook in Roman Social History*. New York: Oxford University Press, 1988.

William G. Sinnigen, ed., *Sources in Western Civilization: Rome*. New York: Free Press, 1965.

Virgil, *The Aeneid*. Trans. Patric Dickinson. New York: New American Library, 1961. Also trans. David West. New York: Penguin Books, 1990.

Modern Sources About Rome's Rise and Roman Civilization

Lesley Adkins and Roy A. Adkins, *Handbook to Life in Ancient Rome*. New York: Facts On File, 1994.

Paul G. Bahn, ed., *The Cambridge Illustrated History of Archaeology*. New York: Cambridge University Press, 1996.

J.P.V.D. Balsdon, *Life and Leisure in Ancient Rome*. New York: McGraw-Hill, 1969.

Mary Beard and Michael Crawford, *Rome in the Late Republic: Problems and Interpretations*. London: Duckworth, 1985.

John Boardman et al., *The Oxford History of the Roman World*. New York: Oxford University Press, 1991.

Brian Caven, *The Punic Wars*. New York: Barnes and Noble, 1992.

Peter Connolly, *Greece and Rome at War*. London: Macdonald, 1998.

Gian B. Conte, *Latin Literature: A History*. Trans. Joseph B. Solodow, rev. Don P. Fowler and Glenn W. Most. Baltimore: Johns Hopkins University Press, 1999.

T.J. Cornell, *The Beginnings of Rome: Italy and Rome from the Bronze Age to the Punic Wars (c. 1000–264 B.C.)*. London: Routledge, 1995.

Tim Cornell and John Matthews, *Atlas of the Roman World*. New York: Facts On File, 1982.

Michael Crawford, *The Roman Republic*. Cambridge, MA: Harvard University Press, 1993.

Jean-Michel David, *The Roman Conquest of Italy*. Trans. Antonia Nevill. London: Blackwell, 1996.

Gavin de Beer, *Hannibal: Challenging Rome's Supremacy*. New York: Viking Press, 1969.

Donald R. Dudley, *The Romans, 850 B.C.–A.D. 337*. New York: Knopf, 1970.

Will Durant, *Caesar and Christ*. New York: Simon and Schuster, 1944.

Jane Gardner, *Roman Myths*. Austin: University of Texas Press and British Museum Press, 1993.

Michael Grant, *History of Rome*. New York: Scribner's, 1978.

——, *The Visible Past: Recent Archaeological Discoveries of Greek and Roman History*. New York: Scribner's, 1990.

——, *The World of Rome*. New York: New American Library, 1960.

Erich S. Gruen, *Culture and National Identity in Republican Rome*. Ithaca, NY: Cornell University Press, 1995.

Sir John Hackett, ed., *Warfare in the Ancient World*. New York: Facts On File, 1989.

R.R. Holloway, *The Archaeology of Early Rome and Latium*. New York: Routledge, 1994.

Antony Kamm, *The Romans: An Introduction*. London: Routledge, 1995.

Robert B. Kebric, *Roman People*. Mountain View, CA: Mayfield, 1997.

Lawrence Keppie, *The Making of the Roman Army*. New York: Barnes and Noble, 1994.

Serge Lancel, *Carthage: A History*. Trans. Antonia Nevill. Oxford: Blackwell, 1992.

J.F. Lazenby, *The First Punic War: A Military History*. Stanford, CA: Stanford University Press, 1996.

Paul MacKendrick, *The Mute Stones Speak: The Story of Archaeology in Italy*. New York: St. Martin's Press, 1960.

Don Nardo, *Encyclopedia of Ancient Rome*. San Diego: Greenhaven Press, 2002.

——, *Life of a Roman Soldier*. San Diego: Lucent Books, 2000.

——, *The Punic Wars*. San Diego: Lucent Books, 1994.

Stewart Perowne, *Roman Mythology*. London: Paul Hamlyn, 1969.

H.J. Rose, *Religion in Greece and Rome*. New York: Harper and Brothers, 1959.

Michael Rostovtzeff, *Rome*. Trans. J.D. Duff. London: Oxford University Press, 1960.

H.H. Scullard, *Festivals and Ceremonies of the Roman Republic*. London: Thames and Hudson, 1981.

Chester G. Starr, *A History of the Ancient World.* New York: Oxford University Press, 1991.

L.P. Wilkinson, *The Roman Experience.* Lanham, MD: University Press of America, 1974.

Terence Wise, *Armies of the Carthaginian Wars, 265–146 B.C.* London: Osprey, 1996.

Index

About the Editor

Historian Don Nardo has written numerous volumes about the ancient Roman world, including *The Collapse of the Roman Republic*, *Life of a Roman Slave*, *Life of a Roman Soldier*, and *Rulers of Ancient Rome*. Most recently, he compiled Greenhaven Press's massive *Encyclopedia of Ancient Rome* and *Encyclopedia of Greek and Roman Mythology*. Mr. Nardo resides with his wife, Christine, in Massachusetts.